Christ in Glory

A handbook for Christian visitors
to the seven churches
of the Revelation of St John

By
John Hayden

Honey Hill Publishing

Honey Hill Publishing
St Mary's Church, Honey Hill, Bury St Edmunds, Suffolk IP33 1RT, UK

ISBN 978-0- 9554504-4-0

Contents

Introduction

The aim of this book is to provide a handbook for Christians visiting western Turkey and especially the Seven Churches that occur in the book of the Revelation. It also provides a background book for any church undertaking a study course on the Seven Churches.

It is recognized that for some this may be the only book they have time to read and so it contains all the key information required. However, it is in a very condensed, even note, form and those visiting are urged to make use of

Guide books of the sites

Good colour guides are available at Ephesus, Pergamum and Pamukkale. Sadly there is little available about other sites,and the information here took a lot of time collating from visits and specialist bulletins.

Bible commentaries

There are two first-rate books on the Seven Churches:

> *The Church under Fire* by Stephen Travis: Bible Reading Fellowship 1995
> *What Christ Thinks of the Church* by John Stott: Candle Books 1990

Reference is made to these in the text and it is hoped that at least one of these will have been read. There are many other Bible commentaries dealing with the church in Ephesus, and I would recommend the commentaries by John Stott in the Bible Speaks Today series by IVP, *The Message of Ephesians, The Message of 1 Timothy and Titus,* and *The Message of 2 Timothy.*

The book is divided into three main sections. **Section A** is designed to be read in the time leading up to the visit. **Section B** is designed to be read during the visit. **Section C** is designed for use at the sites themselves

I am especially grateful for the meticulous editing and proof reading carried out by Lance Bidewell. Try as I might I never managed to avoid many lines getting the red biro treatment!

Bishop John Hayden

(A)
Setting the Scene

The Græco-Roman period

At some time in the second millennium BC, a people called the Dorians invaded Greece and drove out large numbers of Ionians. The Ionians then settled in the Aegean islands and the western coast of Asia Minor. Both peoples were of Greek race, so there were Greeks on both sides of the Aegean.

Beyond the Greek coastal settlements lay the kingdom of Lydia (capital, Sardis) and beyond that various peoples of whom the Greeks knew very little. At the end of the sixth century BC Croesus of Lydia ruled over most of the Ionian Greek cities and sent rich gifts to the mainland Greek shrines, hoping to prevent the mainland Greeks from combining with the Ionians against his rule. In 585BC he went to war against Cyrus of Persia, who had recently extended his territory to the borders of Lydia. He was defeated by Cyrus and the whole of Asia Minor came under Persian rule.

The Persians divided up their empire into satraps, usually ruled by a Persian noble. In 499BC the Ionians attempted to break free from Persian rule and took Sardis. Darius retaliated by invading Greece. Both he and his successor Xerxes were driven back, and after several other battles in 449BC the Greeks in Asia Minor obtained semi-autonomy.

The Greeks were still liable to conscription, and we have an interesting insight into life at the time in the writing of Xenophon. He was hired in 401BC by Cyrus, who was seeking to dethrone the Persian king. Cyrus and all the Greek generals were killed, but Xenophon with others escaped to travel over large areas of present-day Turkey. Xenophon's book, *Anabasis*, opened up for the Greeks the vast expanse of the area.

The southern Greeks regarded the northern Macedonians as barbarians. Philip II, King of Macedonia from 359 to 336, unified Macedonia and built up an army, and was reluctantly appointed by all Greeks to lead an expedition against the Persians to avenge the invasions of Greece. He was assassinated before he started and was succeeded by his son, Alexander, aged 20, who took over Philip's expedition and set out in 334BC. He crossed the Hellespont and fought the battle of Granicus on the plains of Troy which gave him Asia Minor. He went on to conquer an empire stretching from Egypt and Palestine, across Babylon, through Afghanistan to India. He died of fever at Babylon in 323BC.

Alexander's policy to Hellenize the East and spread Greek culture succeeded in large areas of western Asia. By the time of Paul, large areas were Greek in thought and education, even though Greece centred on Athens was in steep decline.

After the death of Alexander the empire was divided among his generals. The Antigonid dynasty ruled in Greece, and western Asia was to be a place of conflict between the Seleucids and the Ptolemy dynasty based in Egypt.

In 191BC the Seleucid Antiochus the Great attempted to free the Greeks from Roman rule by invading Greece. He was defeated and Roman influence spread into Asia. At first the Romans ruled by strengthening the Kingdom of Pergamum. In 133BC Attalus III of Pergamum died and bequeathed his kingdom to the Romans.

The Romans divided the area of Turkey into the provinces of Asia, Bithynia and Pontus, Galatia, Lycia, Pamphylia, Cappadocia and Cilicia. Each had a governor and paid taxes to Rome. For nearly three hundred years there was a time of great prosperity and peace, but towards the end of the third century AD the seeds of later weaknesses were beginning to show. After some major reorganization the empire was divided and Diocletian took the Asian part. He began another severe persecution of the Christians.

In AD323 Constantine took control of the whole empire, and made Byzantium, which he renamed Constantinople, his capital. He rewarded the Christians who had been on his side against their persecutors Diocletian and Licinius. From that time until the Islamic invasion, bishops increasingly held power within local government as the central government went into terminal decline.

Græco-Roman town planning

The first record of town planning was in 3000BC when the Egyptian city of Kahum was built to house the men who worked on the pyramids. The streets were straight and laid out in rectangular blocks. By 500BC city planning was not an unusual procedure. Plans for several Greek cities show radial arteries superimposed on a rectangular system in a fan-shaped design. This form is now used in many countries as a basis for planning new towns.

The Roman town in the provinces was planned round a central forum close to, but separated from, the crossing of two main roads which normally ran north–south and east–west. Less important roads ran at right angles to the main roads. Adherence to this gridiron pattern was so persistent that not infrequently the Romans levelled uneven land to allow straight-line development. They also attempted to segregate industry, and in Rome the height of buildings was limited.

The forum was surrounded by a colonnade and the principal buildings — temples, basilica, senate house and covered market such was the emphasis put on this central area in both Greek and Roman planning, or more correctly, civic design.

Growing complexity of government in the independent cities of the Greco-Roman world necessitated special buildings to be built round the forum. In the *bouleuterion*, or council hall, were the legislative and executive functions. Nearby stood the *prytaneum*, in which was the 'eternal' fire, the official symbol of state unity. Here banquets were held and the General had his residence. Courts were usually held in the colonnades round the forum, the *stoa*, and even in the theatre.

In both civilizations government still retained its ancient connection with religious rites. The Roman temples differed in many important respects from those of the Greeks. Instead of the comparatively low *stylobate*, with its three steps all round, the Romans substituted a high platform, or podium, with a flight of steps on the entrance facade. Also, while Greek temples are isolated from other buildings and almost always face east–west, those of the Romans usually face the forum or are placed at the end of a street to close a vista, their orientation being governed by their relation to other buildings. This results in an emphasis on the entrance facade, with an increased depth to the portico.

During the later Greek period the agora (market place) became a formally enclosed rectangle rather than the picturesque group of colonnades and public buildings. The roads outside the city gates were lined with an ever-increasing variety of sarcophagi.

Baths were a key feature of Roman life and they were of two types: the *balnae*, a type of Turkish bath with rooms at different temperatures, and *therma*, an establishment of great magnificence with facilities for every gymnastic exercise; along with halls for philosophers, poets and rhetoricians. The planning of the therma was governed by axial planning and the grouping of all subsidiary halls and rooms round a great central hall.

Roman private houses were also of two types: the *domus* and *insula*. The domus consisted of suites of rooms grouped round a central hall and was more common in the cities of the eastern Mediterranean. The insulae, or blocks of flats several stories high, were regarded as far too dangerous for an area prone to earthquakes.

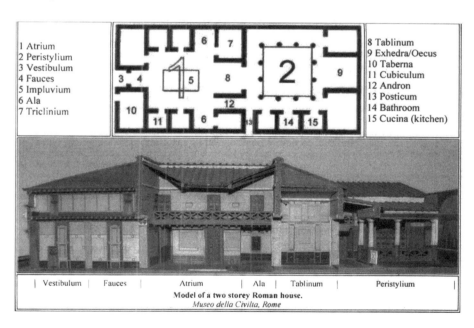

1 Atrium
2 Peristylium
3 Vestibulum
4 Fauces
5 Impluvium
6 Ala
7 Triclinium

8 Tablinum
9 Exhedra/Oecus
10 Taberna
11 Cubiculum
12 Andron
13 Posticum
14 Bathroom
15 Cucina (kitchen)

| Vestibulum | Fauces | Atrium | Ala | Tablinum | Peristylium |

Model of a two storey Roman house.
Museo della Civilta, Rome

The Roman Province of Asia

The messenger taking John's letters to the seven churches may have been using a postal route.

The approximate distances are:

Ephesus - Smyrna 40 miles; Smyrna - Pergamum 50 miles;

Pergamum - Thyatira 55 miles; Thyatira - Sardis 40 miles;

Sardis to Philadelphia 30 miles; Philadelphia - Laodicea 50 miles.

A brief history of the Province of Asia

Habitation dates back to around 7,000BC with increasing evidence from the Hittite empire around the time of Abraham. By the eighth century the kingdom of Phrygia was dominant. About 700BC Lydia, with Sardis as its capital, became the leading power. King Gyges was infamous for his cruelty and is thought to be mentioned in the Bible as Gog (Ezek.38-39 and Rev.20:8). The last and most famous of the Lydian kings was Croesus (560-546BC) who was exceptionally wealthy and conquered the whole area. Herodotus gives an account of his downfall. King Croesus enquired of the Delphic oracle as to whether he should wage war against Cyrus, King of Persia (the king who allowed the Jews to return from exile in Babylon). He was told that if he marched east and crossed the river Halys he would destroy a mighty empire. He did - it was his own. Cyrus defeated him and laid siege to Sardis. Sardis fell through carelessness as we will discover later. The area remained under Persian influence until Alexander the Great crossed the Hellespont in 334BC.

The Greek era The area remained under the control of various successors of Alexander (mainly the Seleucids) until Attalus I (241-197BC) of Pergamum defeated the Gaulish Celts and restricted them to the area of Galatia (Greek for Gaul) in the east. Attalus assumed the titles King and Soter (saviour) and gave his name to the Attalid dynasty. His successors Eumenes and Attalus Philadephus (in whose name Philadelphia was dedicated) built up their empire but at the cost of an alliance with Rome. In 133BC Attalus III bequeathed his kingdom to Rome. The Romans organized their wealthy province of Asia from Pergamum. The rule of the Seleucids and the Attalids had great bearing on this area in New Testament times. Both were great founders of cities. Among these were Laodicea, Thyatira and Philadelphia. They also rebuilt towns like Ephesus and Tarsus. They encouraged Jews to settle in these towns. The Attalids made state religion a key feature of their rule and ascribed divinity to their rulers.

The Roman era The emperor Augustus was widely acclaimed for the peace he brought to the region. The Republican governors had used their power to extort as much money as possible while in office. When Augustus assumed power, this ceased. The Emperors therefore stood between the peace-loving citizens of Asia and financial misery. The area was a mix of peoples with Greek as the predominant language and culture. Roman rule continued to encourage Jewish settlement and there were many flourishing synagogues. These opened the way for Christian mission, especially among the Gentiles who were attracted to the Jewish belief in one God and their high moral code.

Architecture

Greek 700-146BC

Greek architecture of the Hellenic Period has long been recognized as the most beautiful building form yet devised by man. The essentially simple column and beam method of construction formed the basis of this style of architecture, which was used for all temples and important public buildings. This style is thought to have been derived from timber construction methods. The columns, beams and other components were stylized and refined by succeeding generations of artists and craftsmen to a degree which has rarely been equalled and never surpassed in the building forms of subsequent ages.

Marble was readily available for constructing the most important buildings, and the natural beauty of this material, carved with great skill into the structurally pure and well proportioned forms of Greek temples glistening white under cloudless Mediterranean skies, must have afforded a sight of awesome beauty, making it easy to believe that the gods had made their homes on earth.

Greek temples, although basically similar in general shape and construction, nevertheless differed in detail and ornament. Three main types are evident: namely the Doric, Ionic and Corinthian Orders. These are chiefly distinguished from each other by the proportions of the columns and the shapes of the column tops or capitals.

The earliest, simplest and most robust style is the Doric, with examples dating from 640BC. The most famous temple built in this style is the Parthenon at Athens, constructed in the period from 447 to 432BC.

The Ionic Order, with examples dating from 560BC, has columns of a more slender proportion than the Doric and can easily be identified by the remarkable volute, or scroll, design of the capitals.

The Corinthian dates from 420BC. The slender columns are topped by an inverted bell shape surrounded by acanthus leaves.

Roman 146BC – AD365

Remains of buildings dating from the Roman period are to be found at many of the ancient city sites of Asia Minor and Greece.

Roman architecture owes much to the Greeks and also the Etruscans who were the original inhabitants of Central Italy. Their architecture, dating from about 750BC, is specially notable for the use of the radiating arch, and the Romans continued to use this form combined with the column and beam favoured by the Greeks. This combination of columns and beams with arches and vaults gives Roman architecture its own distinctive character.

The Doric, Ionic and Corinthian Orders continued to be used by the Romans, who also added two other types, namely the Tuscan and the Composite. The Tuscan is a simplified version of the Doric with an unfluted shaft, simple moulded capital and plain entablature. The Composite has a capital which is a combination of the Corinthian and Ionic types and was often used in triumphal arches to give an ornate character.

Temples were the predominant buildings of the Greeks and were of one storey, but the complex civilization and varied needs of the Romans demanded other buildings, often of several storeys. Thermae (baths), temples, amphitheatres, aqueducts, bridges, tombs and basilicas all testify to the great constructive ability of the Romans, whose majestic buildings were in accord with the grandeur of Roman Imperial power.

The Romans invented a form of concrete which they used to great effect and economy in the construction of walls, vaults and domes. Brick, stone, marble and mosaic were still used, but only as facing materials.

Mosaics were used not only on walls but on floors and are of great variety. Statues housed in niches in walls were much in use as decoration.

Temples were similar in general form to Greek temples, although half columns attached to the side walls often took the place of the surrounding colonnade of the Greeks. Roofs were often vaulted. They were generally sited to face onto the public open space or forum. A few temples, such as the famous Pantheon in Rome, were built in circular form.

Basilicas were halls of justice and commercial exchange. The usual plan of a basilica was a rectangle twice as long as its width. Two or four rows of columns divided the interior into three or five aisles. The tribunal was at the far end on a raised dais, set in a semicircular apse around which were ranged seats for the assessors. The basilica form is interesting, in that it was adopted by the early Christians as a pattern for church buildings, after Christianity was permitted as a public religion in the fourth century AD.

Greek Capitals

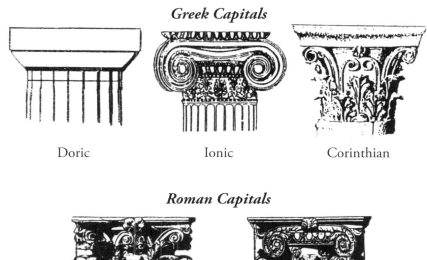

Doric   Ionic   Corinthian

Roman Capitals

Corinthian   Composite

Byzantine AD 324 onwards

The dome, which had always been traditional in the east, became the dominant design feature of Byzantine architecture, which was a fusion of domed with columnar construction. Domes of brick, stone or concrete were supported on pendentives over square compartments, whereas in Roman architecture the use of a dome was limited to compartments of circular or polygonal shape. The use of the dome as the main constructional element governed the plan form of Byzantine churches, which usually consist of a central square space covered by a dome on pendentives and surrounded by short arms on each side to give a cross-shaped plan, the remaining corners being often filled in to complete a square.

An entrance vestibule or narthex was built onto one side to give access to the church, while at the opposite end a semicircular recessed area or apse housed the altar, which was partitioned off from the main body of the church by a screen or iconostasist.

Domes or semi-domes were sometimes used to cover the subsidiary parts of Byzantine churches in addition to the central space. In order to withstand the thrust from the domes, the walls were solidly constructed of brick or stone, with exterior decoration taking the form of banding patterns. Internally, the large areas of wall and dome surface were decorated by marble, glass mosaic and wall paintings. The interior of a Byzantine church was one vast visual aid, illustrating Bible events and Christian doctrine in rich and glowing colours. Figure sculpture was not allowed by the Greek Church as it was regarded as idolatry.

Windows were small, making the interior restful and cool in contrast to the glaring eastern sunshine outside. An encircling ring of windows, set in the base of the dome, was often the chief source of light for the church. Columns were used to support galleries, and in early buildings these were often obtained from existing ancient buildings. When new columns were used, the capitals were of designs developed from the Greek or Roman types, or a new pattern such as the cushion, bird or basket.

The key characteristic of Byzantine ornament is that the pattern is incised rather than raised.

The Byzantine style of architecture was adopted by the Orthodox Church as being eminently suitable for the unchanging forms of its liturgy, and as such has continued as a traditional building type right down to the present day.

Three examples of Byzantine capitals

Islamic AD1453 onwards

When the Ottoman Turks captured Byzantium they inherited a number of impressive churches. These were converted for use as mosques and also served as patterns for new mosques.

The great mosques of Istanbul, built from the sixteenth century onwards, were modelled on the Hagia Sophia, Istanbul which was already 1,000 years old by this time.

Ornament in mosques and other Islamic buildings was strictly regulated by the rules of the Koran, which prohibited the copying of natural objects. In consequence, forms of decoration were developed based on elaborate geometric designs and using brilliant colouring in red, white, blue, silver and gold. Often quotations from the Koran in Arabic script were used as decoration, in the form of tiled panels. In contrast to Greek architecture, which was essentially very simple in form, Islamic architecture is characterized by the intricacy and restlessness of the elaborate geometric ornament, used both internally and externally in mosques and other important buildings.

Fountains, which are often roofed over, are to be found in the forecourts of mosques and in public squares.

Turbes (tombs) are of a unique shape and are to be found near mosques.

An Islamic style capital

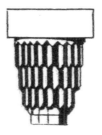

Life in first-century Asia

City Life

The cities were the meeting-places for peoples from many cultures. The Greeks had settled into the area and their own ideas became assimilated with those of the local people. This is very noticeable in the case of religion, where certain local gods are given Greek names. The cities in the area were prosperous. We will see many wide marble streets and the remains of fine buildings—buildings that contrast favourably with those in Greece or Italy. Very little remains of Laodicea, the richest of these cities, but it had three theatres compared with only one elsewhere and could rightly claim to have need of nothing.

Today we find it hard to grasp how city life in Asia was so advanced and prosperous. The better houses had tap water and central heating; and there were street lamps, large sport and recreation facilities, and universities of considerable standing. Pergamum and Ephesus had world-famous libraries comparable in their day to those in the UK. In comparison Athens was in decline, living on past glories, and the rest of Europe seemed barbaric. Yet it was under Roman rule that they flourished. It is said that the Greeks are better and more prosperous under almost any government than they are under their own, but it is probably not wise to point that out to a modern-day Greek!

Commerce

The area, as it is today, had a large agricultural industry and the cities grew wealthy by providing the markets and light industry linked to the surrounding community. Ephesus was also a major port and centre for trade. Roads from all over the area and as far away as India converged on this town and it is quite likely that the description of a market in Revelation is taken from the *agora* (market place) here:

> *cargoes of gold, silver, precious stones and pearls; fine linen, purple, silk and scarlet cloth; every sort of citron wood, and articles of every kind made of ivory, costly wood, bronze, iron and marble; cargoes of cinnamon and spice, of incense, myrrh and frankincense, of wine and olive oil, of fine flour and wheat; cattle and sheep; horses and carriages; and bodies and souls of men.* (Rev.18:12-13)

Christ in Glory - *a handbook for Christian visitors to the seven churches of the Revelation of St. John*

Sardis, too, had a river running through it from which could be panned gold and, like Laodicea and Thyatira, was the centre of a wool and dye trade. The temple of Artemis at Ephesus housed an important deposit bank and Laodicea was a centre for banking. The use of coins for currency was invented in this area. Laodicea also exported its famous eye salve *Tephra Phrygia*.

Government

The Romans allowed these Greek cities considerable freedom. They were ruled by a democratic monarchy so that democratic freedom and autocratic rule tempered and restrained each other. The citizens were united by a common religious bond held in their local god. So Demetrius caused a considerable riot (Acts 19) when he accused Paul of treason to the City god: *Great is Artemis of Ephesus*. He claimed that the unity and reputation of the city was at stake. Indeed it was, and we find that Christianity began to break down the barriers—we are all brothers and sisters in Christ. However, in the first century Christianity was seen as part of the Jewish religion. The Jews belonged to a *religio licita*—a legal religion. It came about like this. The government was keen for Jews to settle and trade in the cities. A city was an association of tribes, so when the Jews were in sufficient numbers they were made into a tribe and could worship their tribal God. They were not required then to go to court or trade on the Sabbath, and when oil or food allowances were given they were allowed to have the equivalent in cash. These privileges, along with the wealth of the Jews, did not help their popularity. From time to time the Greeks attempted to have the Jews expelled, and towards the end of the first century some Jews tried to divert such unpopularity onto the Christians, many of whom, like Timothy, were Jews who had joined the Christian church. At Sardis, sited alongside the gymnasium, there are the remains of a large synagogue, and built along its south wall a series of Jewish-owned shops.

Leisure

In a society based on slavery—and there were usually more slaves than freemen - there was plenty of time for leisure, mental and physical. In Ephesus and Pergamum there were great libraries but all cites had their lecture halls and theatres which were used for drama, music and debate.

The gymnasium provided a place for physical exercise and training for events in the stadium. Gladiatorial shows normally took place in the stadium, not the theatre. A lot of time was also spent at the public baths and relaxing in the various temples or brothels.

Houses, even for the rich town dweller, were not large. They were used mainly for sleeping and eating. Most of the day was spent outside the house.

Spotlight on Ephesus

Ephesus is one of the most important cities of the ancient world and its site is one of the most extensive. The early city grew for two reasons.

a) **Harbour** Here was a natural outlet for trade from the Euphrates and the East, and from the large agricultural area of the Meander valley. Ships sailed to Spain, Italy, Greece, Egypt and the Black Sea. However, soon after New Testament times the harbour silted up. The town declined, and eventually swamps, mud-flats and ruins were left. Seljuk became the main town for the area and Kusadasi became the port.

b) **Temple of Artemis** The temple of the Anatolian mother-goddess was taken over by the Greeks as the Temple of Artemis or Diana. Over the years five temples were built on the site. The temple drew worshippers from a wide area. Kings, states and individuals with treasure or money to deposit banked it here, secure behind the image of Artemis, which may have been a meteorite (Acts 19:35). Images of the goddess have been uncovered and are on show in the Seljuk museum. The last and greatest temple, one of the seven wonders of the world, sank into the swamps. J T Wood of the British Museum unearthed the foundations again in 1870.

By New Testament times Ephesus was the first and greatest city in Asia with a population of around 300,000. The Roman proconsul normally resided in Ephesus although the official capital was in Pergamum. Paul had friends among the Asiarchs (Acts 19:31) whose function was to promote the worship of the Emperor. Ephesus had three temples and, by the time of the Revelation, the seven metre high statue of Domitian dominated the town.

We will look in more detail at the site of Ephesus in a later study. The sketch map overleaf gives an idea of the basic city plan.

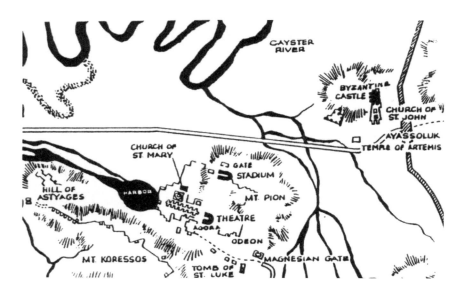

Christians at Ephesus : An overview

Paul's first visit In AD52 (Acts 18:18-21) Paul visits Ephesus at the end of his second missionary journey on his way back to Jerusalem. He leaves Aquila and Priscilla there to begin the church after he had met up with some of the Jews in the synagogue. We know from the Jewish historian, Josephus, that a large number of Jews lived in Ephesus, so Paul would have seen this as a strategic place for future work.

Paul's second visit From AD53-54 (Acts 19) Paul spent two years at Ephesus. During this time the gospel spread throughout Asia. It spread eastward up the Lycus river valley and trade routes to Colossae, Hierapolis and Laodicea, and in the north and east to Smyrna, Pergamum, Thyatira, Sardis and Philadelphia. While in Ephesus Paul wrote several letters to the church in Corinth. He mentions that he fought with 'wild beasts' (1Cor.15:32). It is unlikely that Paul, a Roman citizen, was actually thrown to the lions as there was no venue for such fights, although later the stadium was adapted. More likely he is referring to the behaviour of some of those with whom he was in dispute. At the end of this third missionary journey he calls the Ephesian elders to Miletus. He warns them (Acts 20:16-38) that some of them would distort the truth and urges them to stand firm in their faith.

Paul writes to the church in Asia After his arrest in Jerusalem (AD57) Paul is imprisoned in Caesarea and then at Rome. During this time he wrote several letters to the Asian Christians. We have the epistles to the Ephesians, Colossians and Philemon. It is likely that the epistle to the Ephesians was a letter to all the churches in the area. (The words 'in Ephesus' [Eph.1:1] do not occur in many manuscripts.) The scribe would have replaced the name of the city in v.1 with others such as Laodicea In Colossians 4:16 we read 'After this letter has been read to you, see that it is also read in the church of the Laodiceans and that you in turn read the letter from Laodicea.'

A coin from Ephesus showing the temple of Artemis

Paul's third visit This came after he was released from house arrest in Rome. He had hoped to go west and visit Spain (Romans 15:24,28) but instead he made for Colossae to visit Philemon. He called in at Ephesus and found that his fears about false teaching had come true. So he dismisses Hymenaeus and Alexander from their positions of leadership in the church and leaves Timothy in charge to try and sort matters out.

John moves to Ephesus Sometime after this the apostle John seems to have moved to Ephesus with Mary the mother of Jesus. We do not know why this happened. It could be that Timothy, a young man, found the task too great and so a senior apostle is recruited. The fact is that we do not know, and we cannot be sure that Mary came with him, although there is some evidence for this in the early church. John seems to have been like a bishop to the church in Asia, and later, when he was banished to the nearby Isle of Patmos he wrote to them the letter of Revelation – the last book of the Bible.

The third Council The third General Council of the Christian Church took place at Ephesus in AD431. It condemned the Nestorian doctrine that Christ was really two persons, one human and the other divine. The council sat in the double church of St Mary, the ruins of which are still there to the north of the harbour road.

Mary's house is situated in the hills to the south of Ephesus. There is no early church evidence that this was her home, nor do we know that John was buried in the church at Seljuk. We do know that a major church was built above a grave of John in the early years of the Christian church and that the early church historians, Irenaeus and Eusebius, refer to John's burial there.

The Church of St John The Emperor Justinian built a new magnificent church dedicated to St John. The church is in the shape of a cross with a broad nave,

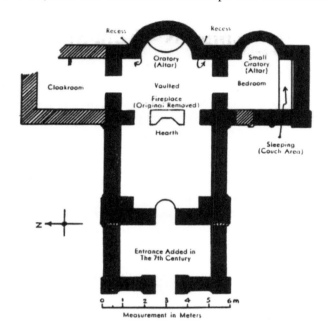

c.

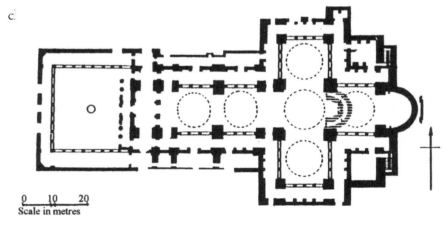

Christ in Glory - *a handbook for Christian visitors to the seven churches of the Revelation of St. John*

Ephesus - from St John onwards

The Roman emperors realised the importance of Ephesus. It, along with Smyrna, Tarsus and Antioch, was a free city, meaning that its internal affairs were governed by its own laws. There were four key trade routes from Rome to the east: i) the sea route from Ostia or Puteoli to Alexandria in Egypt; ii) by land on the Appian way to Brundisium and then by ship to Corinth and beyond; iii) the same as ii) to Corinth and then to Ephesus, and from there through Laodicea and Tarsus to the east; iv) by land to Brundisium, across the Adriatic to Dyrrachium, and then by the Egnatian Way across Macedonia, crossing over into Asia and beyond. The route most frequented by travellers was (iii), so making Ephesus a key port of transit. For most of the first and second centuries Ephesus was the second largest city of the east after Alexandria.

The Emperor Hadrian visited Ephesus twice, and the temple built in his honour is one of the best preserved features in Curetes Street, near the library of Celsus that was built around the same time. The visits of Hadrian saved Ephesus, as they were the incentive to drain the harbour and the swamps of the river Kaystros.

Although in the third century Ephesus maintained its political and religious importance, the seeds of its decline were becoming obvious. The most important event of the century was the destruction of the Temple of Artemis by the Goths, whose main purpose was to plunder its treasury.

In AD431 an event of great importance to Christianity took place in Ephesus. Nestorius of Antioch, while Bishop of Constantinople (AD428-431), stressed the reality of the humanity of Jesus in contrast to those in Alexandria who stressed his deity. Cyril, Bishop of Alexandria, strongly opposed this trend. The Emperor Theodosius II summoned representatives of the church throughout the world to Ephesus for an Ecumenical Council. The council rejected the teaching of Nestorius and adopted the Dogmatic Letter of Cyril, which stated that Jesus was born of a woman; but he did not cast aside his being God. He assumed our flesh; but he continued to be what he was. The council took place in the double church of Ephesus—Hagia Maria Theotokos. Before Christianity became lawful in AD313 the building had been the *Deigma* a clearing-house for the harbour. The 111 general consuls and 200 bishops complained of the bad living condi-

The Virgin Mary and Ephesus

There is good evidence that in the second century there was a church in Ephesus dedicated to the Virgin Mary. The Council of Ephesus met in the double church in 431, as this was the earliest church dedicated to the Virgin. The Bishop of Jerusalem only built a church dedicated to St Mary twenty-eight years after attending this council. Early church historians claim that Mary lived for eleven years at Ephesus and was buried there near the tomb of St John. The house of Mary on a hill overlooking Ephesus was not 'discovered' until a Catholic Sister Catherine Emmerich, who never left Germany, gave remarkably accurate descriptions of the 'house' in the early 1800s. These 'revelations' were followed up in the 1890s by Father Poulain from Izmir, who claimed a house in ruins at Panaya Kapulu fitted the 'revelations'. A church has now been built incorporating the ruins and it has become a major centre for pilgrimage. There are claims of various miraculous cures taking place to those who have drunk the holy water and prayed in the church!

tions and of the unhealthy climate of Ephesus. This was the result of the marshlands caused by the harbour silting up. Yet even at this late time the city was still investing in grand buildings, including the harbour baths, the Arcadian Way and the church in the cave of the Seven Sleepers.

Now came the crunch. To save Ephesus from its impending fate, either the harbour had to be dredged or the city moved towards the coast. Neither was attempted and the once key city of the empire was gradually deserted and fell into ruin.

In the sixth century the Emperor Justinian re-built the Church of St John on a hill above the site of the former Temple of Artemis. Coins have been discovered that show a place of worship existed here from the first century, reinforcing a strong tradition that St John was buried on this site. The church was 110 metres in length—three times the length of St Mary's, Bury St Edmunds! A new settlement grew up round the church and the hill was fortified by walls.

From now on the old Ephesus began to be forgotten and the town was renamed Hagios Theologos (holy theologian) the nickname for St John. The Turks took up this name, calling it Ayasuluk. In a bid to drop all Christian and Greek names, the town is now called Seljuk.

The Turks took possession in 1304 and built the Isabey Mosque and other public buildings, but with the growth of the port of Izmir, Ephesus continued to decline and at the beginning of the twentieth century was an 'unkempt little village of a few houses'. Today Seljuk is a small market town.

(B)
Paul and Ephesus

Paul visits Ephesus

1. Paul the Teacher Acts 19:1-10

The first group of people Paul meets on this visit to Ephesus are those who have heard a little about Jesus but not enough for them to come to faith in Him. Paul makes the point that everyone has to believe personally in Jesus Christ and make a clear-cut decision to follow him. There is no fixed time in our life when this happens. One opportunity is at Confirmation, when, as an adult, we confirm baptismal promises made during our infancy. *When* we make a decision to follow Christ is not as important as making it.

Paul now takes the opportunity to teach the Christian faith. He is able to hire the Lecture Hall of Tyrannus for two years. (Professor F F Bruce comments 'Since *tyrannus* means a despot or tyrant, one wonders idly if this was the name his parents gave him or the name his pupils gave him!') We are not told whether Tyrannus hired his lecture-hall to Paul or whether he freely offered it when he was not using it himself. An early copy of the New Testament says that Paul taught there each day from 11am-4pm. This would mean that Tyrannus used the hall during the normal teaching day, and Paul used it during the extended lunch hour or siesta still common in that part of the world. Keeping to such times may have enabled Paul to earn a basic income from tent-making which Luke mentions in Acts 18:3. Paul's teaching led to many new churches starting throughout the province of Asia (Acts 19:10).

2. Jesus the healer Acts 19:11-16

The good news of Jesus is entering an area which up to now was in the grip of Satan. When Jesus brought the good news of the kingdom to Israel his preaching was linked with miraculous signs. Now 'extraordinary miracles' come with the spread of the word throughout Asia. The use of handkerchiefs (*soudaria*— sweatband for the head) and aprons (*simikinthia*—a waist belt) certainly was extraordinary. Luke wants to stress that God did extraordinary miracles through Paul (Acts 19:11). Again in Acts 19:13 it is made clear that it is Jesus and not Paul who has the power to heal. Paul is the means whereby God can transform lives, spiritually, mentally and physically. Such healings have occurred down the centuries and many have taken place recently in Africa and Asia when the good news of Christ enters areas that were under Satan's rule. As such healings are God at work, we have no control over when or how they take place.

3. The occult Acts 19:17-20

Ephesus was famous in the ancient world for every form of magic, black or white, and occult practice. The ancient world was full of practitioners of the occult who became rich on their claims to cure illness. Near the temple of Domitian in Ephesus there was a large centre specializing in such cures. Plutarch points out that attached to the statue of Artemis were certain symbols, *ta Ephesia grammata,* and these Ephesian letters had been turned into a magical formula. Although the Old Testament expressly forbade dabbling in the occult, Jews were involved. The *Testament of Solomon* even refers to the 'Ephesian letters' and Josephus mentions such practices (Jewish Antiquities 8:45f.). Sceva's sons (Acts 19:14) had not accepted Jesus' moral or spiritual teaching. They had not come to him in repentance and faith. They never claimed to be Christians. Jesus to them was simply the name of some great spirit-power of the world beyond. They had seen the miracles Paul had done and hoped to use the same power for themselves. So they used the words 'In the name of Jesus, whom Paul preaches, I command you to come out' (Acts 19:13). The consequences of this misuse of the name of Jesus is disastrous. The man replies 'Jesus I know, and I know about Paul, but who are you?' (Acts 19:15). 'Galvanised by superhuman strength, the demon-possessed man pounces on them and overpowers them. They receive such a beating that they barely escape with their lives. The magicians, powerless to command the demon, are defenceless against his assault'. (Acts *New Testament Commentary Series*, W.J.Larkin, IVP-USA).

The effect on the believers was to challenge them about their involvement in the occult. They came and confessed they were using charms and secret formulas. The Greek verbs here could mean that they publicly revealed the so-called magical words, so making them useless. They certainly made quite a bonfire (Acts 19:19) worth about £20,000, making sure they did not corrupt others by passing on their magic charms.

> **Handkerchiefs and aprons** Dr John Stott (Message of Acts IVP p.306) makes the following points: a) Luke regards the use of these as extraordinary. b) 'He does not regard them as magic ... which Ephesian believers were soon to confess and renounce as evil'. c) Jesus himself allowed the woman to touch the edge of his cloak (Luke 8:43-44). d) In the Bible demon-possession is distinguished from illness, and therefore exorcism from healing.

Artemis of the Ephesians Acts – 19:23-41

The temple of Artemis was one of the seven wonders of the ancient world. The temple covered an area 130m by 70m and 128 columns 20m high surrounded it. It was four times the size of the Parthenon in Athens. Paul was hoping to stay in Ephesus until the end of May when the annual festival—Artemisia—filled the city with people from all over the region. What better time to reach many for Christ! But his stay was cut short (Acts 20:1).

It was Demetrius, a silversmith, who roused his fellow craftsmen. They were busy making souvenirs of the shrine ready for the annual month-long festival. Yet on their doorstep Paul was urging the people to give up false gods. Demetrius is an independent witness to the effectiveness of Paul's preaching. He had good reason to believe trade would be affected and so did the other craftsmen (Acts 19:24-27).

The agitators rushed from their workshops to the great theatre of Ephesus. At a 'pop' concert in recent times 50,000 packed into the seats. How many came to the call of the silversmiths we do not know, but it seems to have been a large crowd. Paul wanted to defend himself but the Asiarchs advised against this.

The Jews put forward Alexander as a spokesman. He was sent to tell the crowd that it was the Christians who were the cause of the trouble. He may have been Alexander the metal worker to whom Paul refers in 2 Timothy 4:14. The crowd seems to have thought he was the cause. He was howled down, and for two hours the mob chanted 'Great is Artemis of the Ephesians'. Haenchen comments, 'in the final analysis the only thing heathenism can do against Paul is to shout itself hoarse.'

Suddenly the noise dies down. The town clerk has entered and mounts the stage. He looks round at the crowded tiers of marble seats rising up the hillside. He makes a brilliant, typically Greek speech. He points out that the city's reputation as guardian—*neokoros*—of the temple and its image is safe (19:36f); that the Christians have broken no law (19:37); that there are courts and the city council that met three times a month (19:38f) and that unless the crowd disperses peacefully the Roman authorities may regard it as a riot and impose penalties.

Artemis The Ephesians were very proud of this goddess. She was called saviour, queen of the cosmos. Pausanias claims the cult of Artemis or Diana (Latin name) received the highest and most extensive worship in the ancient world, with shrines from Spain to Syria. The conflict here, as it is throughout the Bible, is between home-made gods with their home-made religion and the only true God and his revelation. That is why so much of the Bible is taken up with detailed information about who God is, what he is like, and how we are to worship, love and follow him. The revelation comes from God: it is not invented by man.

> The town clerk—*grammateus*—was the chief executive officer responsible to Rome for law and order. His comment (Acts 19:38) about proconsuls fixes the date at AD54. On Nero's accession. his mother ordered the poisoning of the proconsul Junius Silvanus, so Helius and Celer were acting proconsuls until a successor was appointed.

By contrast, the idols were 'home-made' in more senses than one. The temple, the statues of Artemis (we can see some in the Seljuk museum) and the souvenirs were all man-made. Even if there was a meteorite stone in the temple it certainly bore little likeness to the statues which craftsmen like Demetrius fashioned. It was not only the idols that were man-made; the myths and legends which gave the god importance were also made up. Of course the people didn't see it that way. (One of the frustrating aspects of some guided tours is that the guides concentrate on stories for which they have very little evidence, if any, while failing to explain the key features of the place. Fiction always seems to be more interesting!)

People always prefer the god they can think up that suits their lifestyle. People did it in Paul's day and they do it just as much today. Demetrius' appeal to economic, patriotic and religious motives for the defence of popular religion against the Gospel shows how interrelated are these cultural aspects. Any Christianity worth its salt will be a challenge to the pocketbook, the flag and the shrine. People want to lay down the conditions. We do so today. There is much in the church that is far away from what Jesus taught when it comes to such matters as witness, giving, or care for others. Whether we make a god out of wood or silver or out of our ideas, the great problem is that this god is powerless. The idol will always fail at times of need because it has no power. God will always destroy the false gods and grind them to dust. After years of careful archaeology, all there is to see of the temple of Artemis is one rather battered-looking column re-erected for the tourists and used by the storks as a nesting-place. No one would have heard of Artemis and the wonder of the ancient world if it were not through this encounter with the living God and his destruction of that great shrine. As we visit and look at the remains of the great temple at Ephesus, we are left with a question. Will we follow the God revealed in Scripture or will we make up our own gods, our own pop idols of culture, sport, economics or politics? What idols have we seen come and go in our lifetime?

Paul meets the Ephesian elders – Acts 20:13-38

Paul is on his way to Jerusalem after visiting Greece, and he takes the opportunity to meet up again with the elders from Ephesus. Miletus is a sea port, and the ship would have stayed there two or three days. This was just enough time for Paul to send a runner and for the elders to come down and meet him, but not enough time for Paul to risk leaving the harbour to visit Ephesus himself.

Miletus was a city and seaport about 35 miles south of Ephesus. It is located on the south side of the Meander estuary, the Bay of Latmus. In ancient times it was an important port with four harbours. In the sixth-century BC it was an important centre of art and philosophy (Thales, the first Greek philosopher, and Hecataeus, the historian, lived at Miletus) and established trading colonies as far away as Egypt. It was destroyed by the Persians in 494 BC but by Roman times it had resumed its importance as a trading centre. It was famous for the temple of Apollo at nearby Didyma. The temple covered an area 87m by 41m and had 112 columns 15.45m high. By the time of Paul the harbour was beginning to silt up, and today Miletus (like Ephesus) is five miles from the coast. In the 1930s the traveller H.V. Morton was told it would take ten days to reach Miletus from Izmir across malaria-infested marshes, with no certainty of fording the Meander. Today it is less than an hour's drive from Kusadasi and well worth a visit.

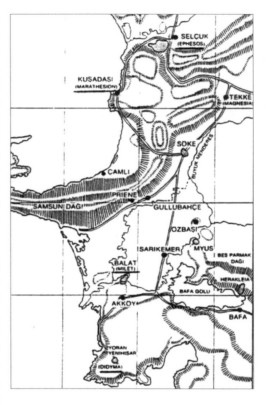

Paul's farewell speech In Acts we have several speeches by Paul to non-Christian audiences. There are three evangelistic sermons (Acts 13, 14 and 17) and five legal defences (Acts 22-26). The farewell address to the elders at Miletus is the only record in Acts of Paul speaking to a group of Christians. It reads like one of Paul's letters. It deals with such themes as grace, the kingdom and purpose of God, suffering, false teachers, watchfulness, redemption, repentance and faith, the church, running the race, and heaven. Notice how Paul concentrates on the example he gave by what he said and did while he was with them. Is our behaviour such that we could urge others to copy us, and in so doing be better Christians?

Luke's account divides into these sections:

a) A review of Paul's past ministry in Ephesus (Acts 20:18-21). Although Paul had only been away for a few weeks, his opponents were already questioning his conduct and teaching. Paul stresses that he did everything in public and his teaching was about the key issues of our faith (Acts 20:21).

b) A statement about his present plan to go up to Jerusalem and personally to take there the famine relief collection (Acts 20:22-24). He realises that such a visit could prove dangerous, and later we read that Paul is arrested while in Jerusalem (Acts21).

c) Paul's future plans (Acts 20:25-27). Paul plans to visit Spain on his fourth journey and so does not expect to return to Ephesus. In fact he did return after his release from house arrest in Rome. This change of plan is good evidence that Luke wrote his Gospel and Acts for Paul's defence in Rome.

d) Warnings (Acts 20:28-31). We are part of God's church to do God's will, not form a club for our own benefit. Archbishop Temple pointed out that the church exists for the benefit of those who are not yet members—we, like Paul, are here to bring others to faith in Christ. When we look at the letters to Timothy we will see that some of Paul's worst fears about the church came true. Major problems led to another visit by Paul, Timothy being sent to take charge, and later the Apostle John being based in the city.

e) Blessing (Acts 20:32). Although Paul must leave them, God was with them and so was his word that was able to build them up and prepare them for heaven.

f) Final exhortation (Acts 20:33-35). Paul urges them to care for the needs of others. He hopes they will follow his example and not expect financial reward.

g) Prayer and Departure (Acts 20:36-38). After prayer and a sorrowful farewell with tears on both sides, Paul and his travelling companions board the ship. Note that Paul is not afraid to show his feelings—tears are mentioned several times—and at the end there was much weeping and embracing. Farewells are sad, but farewells between Christians are never final.

Paul writes to Ephesus

Ephesians 1 – Focus on God

We often take love for granted. We just assume that our parents, our wife or husband, brother or sister love us and take little time thinking about how much their love for us costs them. Why do some parents spend many hours each day being a taxi service or a caterer for their children? Because they love them. Do we show that we appreciate such love?

> Alongside the library of Celsus leading to the Agora in Ephesus is the gate of Mazeus and Mithridates. The gate is 16 metres high with three arches. It was built by ex-slaves Mazeus and Mithridates to express their thanks to the Emperor Augustus (the Emperor at the time when Jesus was born), Empress Livia and daughter Julia for their forgiveness and granting them their freedom.

Paul begins his letter to the Ephesians by focusing on God. What has God - Father, Son and Holy Spirit—done for us? Paul points out that God loves us so much he wants us to enjoy the very best. So he offers us the opportunity to live with him for ever in heaven. Paul asks us to remember three facts.

God chose us (Eph.1:4) We and others who are Christians are so because God loved us before we loved him. God took the initiative. The people of Ephesus were very proud to be the guardians of the temple of Artemis. They were pleased that the Roman governor normally stayed in Ephesus even though Pergamum was the official capital. Paul points out that these good things would not last. They should be even happier in that God has chosen them to experience his love now and for ever with every spiritual blessing (Eph.1:3).

If we accept God's offer we need to enter into a new relationship with him. Sometimes this is referred to as being born again (John 3—Jesus and Nicodemus). Here Paul says it is like being adopted as his son. Half the people living in Ephesus were slaves. Sometimes a master would become very fond of a slave and adopt him or her into his family. In the eyes of the law he or she was a new person; and all records linked to the time in slavery were cancelled. Sometimes the adopted slave even inherited his master's wealth and rank. These slaves realised they did not deserve such a privilege. Paul points out that we do not deserve

God's love or his adoption of us into his family. God's undeserved favour in this way is what Paul calls *glorious grace* (Eph.1:6). How did God enable us to enter his family? It all centres around what Jesus Christ has done for us.

Jesus Christ redeemed us Redemption was a very important word for the half of the population of Ephesus who were slaves. Some slaves would work extra hard, moonlight or indeed do anything they could to save up enough to buy their freedom. Very few ever achieved it. The price was far beyond what they were able to pay. Think what it was like being a slave in Ephesus; think about being forced to do many things that you hated; think about meeting up with other slaves and discussing how you were getting on with saving up to buy your freedom/redemption.

Each day as you go through that gate to market, Paul could have said, 'Remember how grateful these slaves were and how much more grateful we should be to God for our redemption.' We may spend our life here on earth in a difficult situation. Our body, our home or our work may not be up to scratch, but the most important fact to remember is that we are not stuck in that situation for ever. Jesus has come and paid the price for our redemption. One day, slave or free, indeed whoever we are, we will enjoy the benefits of God's children in heaven. There is an old song used by the slaves in America that could well have been sung by the many Christians who were slaves in Ephesus:

> *This world is not my home, I'm just a passing through,*
> *My treasure is laid up, somewhere beyond the blue.*

So what does Paul mean by redemption? Redemption for a Christian means freedom from the power as well as the penalty of sin. We can think of people who are hooked on drugs, alcohol or cigarettes. Once hooked they cannot escape and they destroy their bodies, sometimes gradually, or sometimes in a matter of minutes. Paul says that we are all in the grip of, slaves of, sin and only God can free us. Jesus did this when he died for us on the cross. He paid our penalty and broke the grip of evil. He set us free and he forgave us. For many this was a mystery but for Christians it was an open secret. The solving of any mystery provides endless fascination, none more so than the mystery of God's dealing with humankind. But how can we be sure this redemption will last and that we shall not find ourselves slaves of sin once more? Remember that God the Father chose us, God the Son redeemed us, and now Paul reminds us of the work of the third person in the Godhead.

God the Holy Spirit The Holy Spirit seals us. In Ephesians 1:13-14, Paul writes that we are *marked in him with a seal, the promised Holy Spirit, who is a deposit guaranteeing our inheritance.* The Ephesians would often see such seals. Letters were sealed. Jars of oil and other items also were sealed. Seals were there to remind those who saw them that the article was genuine or the property of the owner of that seal. The seal of the Holy Spirit reminds us that we are genuine Christians and belong to God, in the same way that an engagement ring signifies that the person who wears it is already engaged to be married. God the Father chose us, God the Son forgives and redeems us, and the Holy Spirit in our life is a constant reminder that we belong to God and he will not leave us.

Ephesians 2 – A change of status

Your passport describes you as a British citizen. In some areas of the world such citizenship is highly prized. In the world of the New Testament, Roman citizenship was of similar status. Paul was a Roman citizen and was well aware of the privileges it gave to him. We find one such instance in Acts 22:25-29. We could also be described as citizens of our home towns, even more so if we were born in them. Paul was proud to be a citizen of Tarsus, a university city (Acts 21:39). Only about one in four of those who lived in Ephesus were citizens of that city. Some were slaves; others were *xenoi* or foreigners (xenophobia means fear of foreigners); others were *paroikoi* (resident aliens) who paid taxes and worked but never had voting rights. The citizens of Ephesus always regarded such people as on the fringe and sometimes sought to have them expelled. In most countries such feelings are never far away today. In Ephesians chapter 1 Paul has likened becoming a Christian to a slave becoming a freeman. Now in Chapter 2 he goes a stage further. We may be resident aliens in this world, but we are citizens of heaven and such citizenship is unsurpassed by any in this world (Eph. 2:19).

In Greek or Roman times a citizen had the right of access to the very top. Paul, as a Roman citizen, could claim to be tried by the Emperor himself (Acts 25:10-12). The *Prytaneum* or town hall of Ephesus was a place of major importance. The central portion was flanked by different rooms used for meetings of the town councils. The holy of holies of the city was the inner hall where the sacred fire burned day and night on a central black stone altar. The fire was tended by priests named *kuretes* and by vestal virgins chosen from members of the noble families. Only citizens could enter such a sacred place. Paul's references in Ephesians chapter 2 to the destruction of barriers did not relate only to the relationship between Jews and Gentiles. Jews, along with most people living in Ephesus, were not citizens. They knew the stigma which that brought. Now all Christians are on an equal basis - citizens of heaven. Citizenship means access (Eph.2:18). In prayer we can enter the presence of God.

Paul contrasts the Christian's new status with our former state (Eph.2:11-22). He is thinking primarily about the difference between God's chosen people the Jews, with their opportunity to enter God's presence in the Jerusalem temple, and the Gentiles who were excluded. One of the reasons why Paul was in prison was because the Jews in Jerusalem had accused him of bringing a non-Jew into the temple. For a Jew, the non-Jew was excluded from citizenship as a foreigner to the covenants, without God and without hope. Where God is concerned, that exclusion experienced by non-citizens is true for everyone. Sin has separated every person, of whatever race or nationality, from God. But now Jesus has broken down the dividing wall. Jesus has given people from every race and nationality the opportunity to enter God's presence through what he did on the cross. *His purpose was to create in himself one new person out of the two, thus making peace ... through him we both have access to the Father by one Spirit* (Eph.2:15-18).

Some of the Ephesian Christians were Jews. They had been to Jerusalem for one or more of the great Jewish festivals. They had seen Herod's magnificent temple dominating the city of Jerusalem. They knew all about the divisions between Jew and non-Jew. Paul is speaking to them when he points out that though Christ all races and nationalities have equal access to God.

Paul sums up this new oneness and access with the picture of a new holy temple. John Stott comments, 'As Paul was dictating his letter, there stood in Ephesus the magnificent marble temple of Artemis, one of the seven wonders of the world, and in whose inner shrine there was a statue of the goddess. At the same time in Jerusalem there stood the great Jewish temple built by Herod the Great, barricading itself against the Gentiles, and now also against God, whose shekinah glory it had housed in its inner sanctuary for centuries, but whose glory as revealed in its Messiah it had sought to extinguish. Two temples, one pagan and the other Jewish, each designed by its devotees as a divine residence, but both empty of the living God. For now there is a new temple, *a dwelling place for God in the Spirit*. It is his new society, his redeemed people scattered throughout the inhabited world. They are his home on earth. They will also be his home in heaven. For the building is not yet complete. *It grows into a holy temple in the Lord*. Only after the creation of the new heaven and the new earth will the voice from the throne declare with emphatic finality: "Behold , the dwelling of God is with men".' (*The Message of Ephesians*, IVP, pp 109-110).

Think of yourself sitting with other Christians in Ephesus and listening to Paul's letter. You know all about being citizens and non-citizens, about the divisions between Jews and non-Jews. Certainly you know all about temples—the streets of Ephesus were lined with them and the temple of Artemis made your city famous. Yet Paul has a revolutionary message. Those barriers—Christ has broken them down. Each one of you, whatever your nationality, can become a citizen of God's kingdom on earth and in heaven. What is more, God is not to be found in the great temples but alive in you. You are the new and living temple.

Ephesians 2 & 4 – A new family

The Christians in Ephesus came from different nationalities and social background but a dramatic change took place when they entered the family of God. They became brothers and sisters in Christ with one Father in heaven. How should that change the way they lived? A few months earlier, while staying at Ephesus, Paul had written to the church in Corinth. 1 Corinthians 12 sets out in detail what Paul is going to say to the church at Ephesus. There can be little doubt that the teaching which Paul put in his letter from Ephesus, he also taught to the Ephesian Christians. That is why his reference to certain facts in this letter is in note form. Paul is reminding them of what he had taught during his two years with them. So to understand Ephesians 4 it is best to read I Corinthians 12:12-31. Here are some of the key phrases:

> 'The [human] body is one unit ... though all its parts are many, they form one body ... we were all baptized by one Spirit into one body—whether Jews or Greeks, slave or free...God has arranged the parts in the human body, every one of them [ear, eye, nose, etc.], just as he wanted them to be. ... so that there should be no division in the body, but that its parts should have equal concern for each other. ... Now you are the body of Christ, and each one of you is a part of it. And in the church God has appointed first of all apostles, second prophets, third teachers ... those able to help others, those with gifts of administration ... '.

Now in Ephesians Paul reaffirms the teaching he has given them. He sets out, this time in writing, the reason why Christians should regard themselves as one world-wide family.

Seven facts found in Ephesians 4:4-6

1. One body (Eph.4:4, 15-16). Christ is the head of his body, the church.

2. One Spirit. The Holy Spirit lives in the life of every Christian and, as there is only one Holy Spirit, all Christians are united by him.

3. One hope. God has made the same promises to all Christians. We all have God with us now and we will all share the heavenly home.

4. One Lord. As a sign that one had accepted the Christian faith each person publicly had to say, 'Jesus is Lord'. To us that does not mean very much, but in Ephesus it meant that they were becoming citizens of a new kingdom and their new supreme ruler was Jesus. The Roman Caesar was no longer 'Lord'. Fifty years after Paul the Romans used this test: Who is Lord - Jesus or Caesar? Say 'Caesar is Lord' or die.

5. One faith. Every person can only become a Christian through faith in what Jesus has done for us.

6. One baptism. All are baptized in the name of God—Father, Son and Holy Spirit. Even to this day any person who is not baptized in this way is not regarded as a member of the Christian church.

7. One God and Father. All believers are part of one family and so all can truthfully use the words Jesus taught us and call him, 'Our Father'.

The people of Ephesus knew all about conquering kings and generals who took away people into captivity and demanded ransom and tribute from those whom they had conquered. Psalm 68:18 refers to such a conqueror. He marches in triumph through the streets with his prisoners in chains, whilst his troops carry the precious ransom and tribute he has exacted. Here is the procession of a conqueror.

Paul changes the words of this Psalm (Eph. 4:8) so that the captured end up with the gifts. Now that would have meant a lot to the people of Ephesus. Ephesus had been taken by Alexander the Great, but unlike most other places he conquered, Alexander gave freedom to the city of Ephesus and did not take any tribute. Indeed, he offered Ephesus gifts to restore the temple of Artemis and all taxes collected in the city were used for the benefit of the city and not sent to the ruling power. Through the gifts of Lysimachus, the general who succeeded Alexander, Ephesus became so prosperous that it continued to be the most important city in the Province of Asia for 500 years. Now, teaches Paul, what happened to Ephesus is what has happened to us who have accepted Jesus as our Lord, Master, or King. Instead of taking us off to live a miserable life in captivity and taking everything we had as tribute, he has actually freed us and, what is more, he has given us some wonderful gifts. The gifts have not been used to restore a pagan temple but to make us like gold and precious stones in God's temple. There at the temple of Artemis was the so-called 'tree of life' that was supposed to give paradise (Rev.2:7). In Christ the Garden of Eden is restored and all who come to Jesus can eat of the only tree that gives eternal life (Gen.3:22). These gifts of the conquering Christ are gifts of eternal consequence but they also are gifts enabling us to live for him here on earth. In Ephesians 4:11 Paul mentions *apostles,* who were those who had seen Christ alive and were sent by him to tell others the truth of the resurrection; *prophets,* who had been given true messages by God; *pastors and teachers,* to care for and teach the new members of Christ's family so that it could grow up to be what God had planned it to be. *From Christ the whole body, joined and held together by every supporting ligament, grows and builds itself up in love, as each part does its work* (Eph.4:16). Is that a good description of us?

Ephesians 5 – light or darkness

People live in many different ways. The Bible stresses that, ultimately, all people either live in the light or in darkness. Paul in Ephesians chapters 4 and 5 contrasts these two worlds.

The world of darkness is (Ephesians 5:11-12)

unproductive Looked at through Christian eyes the works of this world are producing nothing that will last. Life without God is like a tree which produces lots of colourful blossom but never any fruit.

secretive A lot of effort goes into trying to make sure that what is thought, said or done is kept secret. Unfortunately for those concerned, the truth sometimes leaks out.

shameful Being caught leads to shame and a loss of respect by others, but the deeds themselves are often shameful and destroy the self-respect of those involved in them.

Action is needed (Ephesians 5:14)
It is easy for those living without God to become complacent: 'It will never happen to me'; 'I will do something about God later'; 'Everyone does it, why should not I?'. Yet no one can be certain what will happen tomorrow. Tomorrow may be too late to repent. Jesus only refers to one person as a fool. Read about him in Luke 12:13-21.

The world of light (Ephesians 5:8-10)
transformation 'You were once darkness, but now you are light in the Lord.' Paul has explained the radical change that takes place in our lives—born anew; and in our status— adopted into God's family and citizens of his kingdom. He now stresses how big a change that is in our day-to-day lives. Some months earlier the Ephesians had made a bonfire of their magic books and charms. Getting rid of that evil had proved costly. There were other habits and attitudes that also needed putting on the 'bonfire'. Entering the family of God involves transformation.

obligation The Ephesians knew all about what it meant to be a member of a household either as a child or a slave. Paul regarded being a Christian as that of being a servant or slave of God. In Ephesians 6:5-8 he describes how slaves should behave. We find he also applies those motives of respect, sincerity and honesty to our relationship with God.

visible In contrast with those who want to keep their actions secret, the Christian is happy that what he does is seen by all. We are children of the light, and happy that the light of God shines through us so that all people can see a life of goodness, righteousness and truth (Eph.5:9).

Earlier in Ephesians 4:17-24 Paul has looked at this matter by contrasting good and evil. In Ephesians chapters 5 and 6 Paul applies the principles of living in the light to family life. We need to remember that there was great variety within Ephesian family life, as was true throughout the world of those days.

Slaves About half the population of Ephesus were slaves. Life for them depended very much on their masters. They may have been brought to the slave market in Ephesus from a distant country and unable to use Greek, the common language of the city. They may have been given dirty and dangerous tasks. At the opposite extreme there were highly educated slaves who acted as private schoolmasters to the household. Just as slaves varied, so did their treatment. Legally they had no rights and some masters were very cruel and abused them, but other masters treated them as if they were their own children.

Resident aliens in Ephesus also came from many countries and brought a great variety of customs with them. Among the resident aliens was a large community of Jews. They continued to keep certain customs linked to their faith. They would not work on the Sabbath, eat certain foods, or go to certain buildings that had links with the pagan gods. They tended to build their houses and businesses in a certain area of the city. They were often wealthy and had many slaves working for them.

Citizens were a small minority. They were usually wealthy, with slaves to do much of the work. The man would spend a lot of the day at the public baths or in the various public buildings discussing and negotiating deals. The woman would run the house and take a slave with her to market to carry back the shopping. The children of the household would be looked after by a slave called a *paidagogos*. He gave some teaching, but his main task was to take you to school, bring you home and make sure you had all your needs.

When Paul wrote his letter he was writing to Christians who belonged to these social groups. What changes do you think were involved in their becoming Christians? What would it be like if you were the only Christian in a household? Think how you would be able to live out your Christian life if you were a slave, or a member of the Jewish community, or a citizen who had previously worshipped Artemis and the other gods whose temples were on all the main streets. How could you live as a member of Christ's world of light? See the comment of Ephesians 5:8-10.

Ephesians 6 – the armour of God

The sight of a Roman soldier was not as commonplace as it was in Palestine. Rome kept its troops near the frontiers of the empire or in 'hot spots' like Judea. Roman soldiers in Ephesus would have been in transit to such areas, or part of a small guard for the proconsul. The city of Ephesus had its own 'police force' and they were very proud that they could keep order without the help of the foreign soldiers. However, everyone knew the uniform of a Roman soldier and Paul uses this as a means of teaching the Christians of their need to stand firm for God.

Paul has no doubt about the outcome of the spiritual battle. He knows that the devil and all evil are defeated, but he also knows that the fight is not yet over. Paul urges us to know that the enemy is spiritual; that God has provided us with the resources for the struggle. Indeed his equipment is more than adequate for the task if we use it correctly.

The armour of God (Eph.6:10-18) is the panoply, which is the full armour of a heavily armed soldier. It has five defensive items and one attacking item. We are to use them in a positive way - put on, stand, buckle, fit, take.

The belt of truth (6:14) The belt bound the long loose clothes under the armour to free the soldier for action. The armour might look good, but if the belt was not in place underneath, in the heat of battle disaster could strike. As a Christian, it is not adequate just to appear good on the outside: we need the integrity and truth of Christ's standards to be able to stand firm. When things get tough wrong things in our lives are too often exposed.

The breastplate of righteousness (6:14) This key item of armour protects the heart and lungs. Being right with God is *not* an optional extra for certain saint-like Christians. It is for all Christians. Sins are chinks in the armour. Right actions and a clear conscience give us vital protection.

The sandals of the gospel of peace (6:15) Military sandals, like the military boot of today, were made to stand up to hard wear, giving a good grip on the long marches as well as on the battlefield. The Roman *caliga* (half-boot) was made of leather, had heavy studded soles, and was firmly tied to the ankles and shins. We all know what it is like when we are walking on ice or mud. We are never sure when we will slip. Having shoes on is a sign that we are up and ready for action. We can put on a coat as we move forward but we can't tie up shoe-laces and run at the same time! Christians need a God given peace of mind so that they have confidence and readiness for action in their daily march against the evil one. That peace comes through our relationship with Christ.

The shield of faith (6:16) The *scutum,* a long oblong shield measuring 1.2m by 0.75m, was able to guard the Roman soldier against the darts and spears of the enemy, but it had to be used in a special way. One on its own was not big enough to provide total protection. In battle the Roman foot soldiers formed a phalanx. The first row of soldiers knelt on one knee, placed their shields on the ground and locked them together. The next row placed their shields on top, and so did the rows of soldiers after them. The enemy was faced with a solid wall of armour. There was only one way through and that was by a soldier failing to hold his ground. In this whole passage of Ephesians, Paul is writing in the plural. Just as earlier in his letter he has taught that we are to see ourselves as part of one body, so now we are not to be lone soldiers fighting individual battles, like gladiators in the stadium, but a disciplined army. We all stand firm together because we all can know the truth revealed by Jesus and put our trust, confidence and faith in him.

The helmet of salvation (6:17) This is the last of the protective armament. Satan will attack the brain, and in psychological warfare seek to put doubts in our minds that will cost us the battle before it has begun. Christian are saved because of what Jesus did for us. He died that we might be forgiven. If we think we will be saved and make it to heaven by being good and doing more good than bad, then there will always be a doubt in our minds—are we good enough? The answer is that we will never be good enough for God; we don't have to be. We wear the helmet of salvation that Christ has provided. So in spite of our failures we can be sure nothing can separate us from God's love (Rom. 8:35-39).

The sword of the Spirit (6:17) The sword is the only offensive weapon. The 'word' here is the spoken word. We can keep our swords sharp by reading our Bibles regularly and learning our faith so that when faced by those who oppose God we can go on the attack. How much do we know, and can we, with confidence, put it across to others?

Paul writes to Timothy – 1

Paul's letters to Timothy give us some idea of the last years of his life. Paul was released from house arrest in Rome in AD63 and set out once more on his travels. He visited Ephesus and left Timothy there to look after the church in the area. Paul seems to have been arrested again and wrote to Timothy in AD66 urging him to come to Rome. In AD67 Paul was beheaded during the persecution of Christians by the Emperor Nero. Paul's letters to Timothy give us many details about life in the church at Ephesus. We will concentrate on some of these. As we do so we need to ask, how has church life changed?

Church
From the very beginning Christians formed themselves into groups and met together for worship. When Jews met together they formed a synagogue and some early Christian groups used that name. The early Christians also used the word *ekklesia* (church) and this gradually took over from 'synagogue' towards the end of the first century to show that there was a difference between Judaism and Christianity. In the Greek world the *ekklesia* are those citizens who are called together by a herald to form an assembly. In I Timothy 2:7 Paul points out that God appointed him to be a herald to call all people into the assembly of God's people. The early Christians felt that they were being called out of the world to form the people of God.

Where did they meet?
We know that during his stay in Ephesus Paul was able to use the lecture hall of Tyrannus (Acts 19:10). We do not know if this room was still available to the Christians after Paul left. It is more likely that the Christians met in various homes as was the custom elsewhere. We know that there were many wealthy members in the Jewish community and some of these would have become Christians. People would have crowded in, sitting on the floor and even on window sills (Acts 20:9), leaning against the walls and any other suitable place. Even fairly small houses, which in those days had few items of furniture, could accommodate large numbers. In Acts 2 there seemed to have been 120 people in a Jerusalem house.

What did they do at their meetings?

Prayer At an *ekklesia* of the city of Ephesus, prayers were usually offered for the Emperor and other leaders before the start of the assembly (to this day similar prayers are offered in our Parliament and at town council meetings) and each speaker would also offer a short prayer before he began to speak. In 1 Timothy 2:1-7 Paul urges Christians to follow this practice in their *ekklesia*. Then in 1 Timothy 2:8 he encourages them to lift up holy hands in prayer. Lifting up one's hands in prayer was a Jewish custom. We find an interesting example of this in Exodus 17:8-16. The Israelites were fighting the Amalekites, and gained ground whenever Moses lifted up his hands and prayed. When he became tired, he sat down, and Aaron and Hur supported his arms. Moses built an altar as a reminder that hands were lifted up to the throne of the Lord. Christians may also have adopted this stance in praying as a reminder of how Jesus hung on the cross.

Praise In Ephesians 5:19-20 Paul urges the Christians at Ephesus: *Speak to one another with psalms, hymns and spiritual songs. Sing and make music in your heart to the Lord, always giving thanks to God.* Obviously singing and giving thanks were not just for when the Christians came together, but we can be certain this formed part of their worship if the neighbours did not object too strongly! Paul points out that it is what Christ has done, is doing, and will do for us which makes us feel so happy that we want to sing. The Christians were dazzled with the wonder that God loved them and would never leave them or forsake them. Do we sing with joy and enthusiasm? If not, is it because we have not discovered God in a real and living way?

Participation When Paul was in Ephesus he had written to the Corinthians about their participation in worship, and in 1 Corinthians 11:17-34 he refers to the Lord's Supper. Christians at Ephesus came from both Jewish and Greek backgrounds and in each culture this meal together was very significant. For the Jews the common meal was linked, as it was for the disciples in the Upper Room, with the Passover. Here was a time when they remembered how God had saved them from slavery in Egypt (Exod.12). The Passover meal had many rituals and some of these were carried into the life of the early church. In the many pagan temples of Ephesus, devotees of a pagan god and trade guilds connected with it would meet together for a meal, eating food sacrificed to that idol (1 Cor.10:20-22). Like the Israelites of old (Exod.24:11), those who attended these meals in the pagan temples regarded this as an important act of communion or fellowship. We do not have any evidence from the New Testament that the Ephesian Christians linked the token meal of bread and wine, remembering the sacrifice of Christ on the cross, with an agape (sharing their evening meal together) but this may well have happened in some of the house churches. Today in many churches, especially in the USA, Christians spend most of Sunday morning together sharing breakfast and sometimes lunch. This helps to build up a church family. How can we build up this spirit of being God's family?

Paul writes to Timothy – 2

Life in the Christian community

Paul concentrates much of his letter on helping the Christians at Ephesus to *know how they ought to conduct themselves in God's household, which is the church of the living God.* Christians came from many cultural backgrounds and social classes. It was very hard for them to work out Christian standards of behaviour. Paul tackles some issues. There are others that he mentions elsewhere but these were important to the church at Ephesus. All Christians should live such lives and certainly no one is to be appointed as a leader unless he or she is setting a good example in these matters. How do they relate to church life today? (All references are from 1 Timothy.)

a) *Above reproach* (3:1), *having a good reputation* (3:7) and *worthy of respect* (3:8) It was important that there was no defect of character or conduct in past or present life which could be used to discredit them either in or outside the church.

b) *Sincere* (3:8) They should not say one thing to please one person and the opposite to please another.

c) *Married and managing children and household* (3:2, 4 & 12) There are various interpretations to this, and this may have been so in Paul's day when Christians came from such a broad mix of people. Certainly Paul is urging faithfulness in marriage, with the husband and wife bringing up their children in a Christian way and the wife, who normally managed the household affairs, keeping a home which honours God. A chaotic home life suggests an inability to provide leadership where others are concerned.

d) *Temperate* (3:2), *not indulging in much wine* (3: 3 & 8) Although alcohol was put in water as a safety measure in a time when there was no clean drinking water, alcohol was abused then as it is now and became a drug. Whatever the drug that causes addiction, and alcohol is not the only one, addiction is not the Christian way. It is wise to err on the side of caution.

e) *Self-controlled* (3:2) This was a virtue stressed by the great Greek philosophers like Socrates and Plato. Christians should have control over their passions and desires. *Respectable* (3:2) means well behaved. Self-control produces outward dignity.

f) *Without anger or dispute* (2:8), *not violent but gentle* and *not quarrelsome* (3:3) Some people are far too trigger-happy, always looking for a fight. Instead, Christians are urged to be patient, putting up with others, ready to forgive.

Women in the church

Paul has to give some extra teaching about the role of women in the church. In Roman culture a few women attained considerable power and influence in a variety of roles: within the home, and outside it in civic, religious and business life. In both Jewish and Greek culture the woman's primary place was to manage the household (1 Tim.5:14). Apollodorus describes the situation: 'We have *hetairai* for pleasure, wives to bear children and to be trusted guardians of things in the house.' The *hetairai* provided companionship and entertainment for men at the temple parties. Jewish women were not as restricted in public appearance as Greek women but did not have the freedom of Roman women. Many of the physical household duties of the Jewish women in Ephesus, like cooking and laundry, would have been done by slaves, as most Jews were in that strata of society. Her influence in the family was considered greater than the man's. In the Jewish synagogue the women were separated from the men and did not lead worship or teach. In 1 Timothy 5:9-10 Paul gives the Christian standard for a woman. She should be faithful to her husband, and well known for her good deeds, such as bringing up children, showing hospitality, helping those in trouble.

The early church faced a major problem trying to give women a role in the church worship that would satisfy these different cultural backgrounds. It was important that neither those who came to worship nor those who rejected the Christian message were offended by what happened in church life and especially in worship. With strong Greek and Jewish influence at Ephesus, Paul teaches that women should avoid giving offence to either of these cultures.

It was important that Christian wives from the Greek homes did not behave in church in any way that might be interpreted that they were *hetarai*. So Paul, knowing how the *hetarai* appeared in public, advises in 1 Timothy 2:9, that

Christian women *are to dress modestly, with decency and propriety, not with braided hair or gold or pearls or expensive clothes.* Likewise, bearing in mind Jewish synagogue worship, Paul does not permit women to teach or have authority over a man.

Leaders in the church should be *able to teach* (3:2) as their duties could include preaching and teaching (5:17) and their teaching needed to come from a good knowledge of the Bible (3:9). Two dangers are highlighted. They should not be *recent convert*s (3:6) as there was a danger that over-rapid promotion would lead to pride. They also should not be in it for the money (3:8). Paul had always set a good example in this respect. He had worked as a tent maker so that he was no charge on the church.

Paul writes to Timothy – 3

In his second letter to Timothy, Paul compares being a Christian to life as a soldier, an athlete, a farmer and a road maker. Let us see what these pictures meant to Christians in Paul's time and what they mean today.

A soldier (2 Timothy 2:3-4) The Greek philosopher Epictetus pointed out that the life of every man is a kind of campaign, and a campaign that is long and varied. To be a soldier in Paul's time meant total commitment. Paul points out that soldiers know all about enduring hardship: only about half survived their twenty years of tough service to reach retirement. Soldiers were not allowed to have any civilian links: they were certainly not allowed to marry and have family ties. Their whole focus had to be on obeying their commanding officer. When he joined the army a soldier took the *sacramentum,* the oath of loyalty. In its rules for priests the Roman Catholic church has adopted many of the conditions laid down for soldiers. The best known rule is that they are not allowed to marry. In the past married people tended to have a child every two years or less. In no way could Paul have travelled as he did with one child on his shoulders, leading another by the hand, while his wife led a couple more! Many Roman Catholics feel that times have changed so that this rule could be relaxed. John Stott points out that 'what is forbidden for us as a good soldier of Jesus Christ is not all activities outside the church—home, work, sport, etc.—but rather *entanglements* which, though they may be perfectly innocent, like playing football, may hinder our Christian lives'. What entanglement is there in my life that comes before my obeying my heavenly commanding officer?

An athlete (2 Timothy 2:5) The Greek words used by Paul, *athlein nomimos,* are those used of a professional athlete. The intense discipline and training were well known. Before taking part in major games like the Olympics, even amateur athletes had to pledge ten months of hard training, all to try and obtain a winning garland, not riches like our modern-day athletes. The spare-time Christian is a contradiction in terms; our whole life is so to live out the faith that we finish the race (2 Tim.4:7-8). Keeping the rules is vital in athletics; that is as true today as it was in Paul's day. Some athletes must not put even part of a foot wrong - the sprinter on the blocks, the long-jumper, the shot- putter are good examples. Living the Christian life like an athlete is rather like running the marathon. It involves long-term training, and when we are running, it is important we keep up the necessary nourishment of learning from God's word, like the marathon runner taking regular refreshment. There will be times when it feels as though we are constantly running uphill and we forget that we have just run downhill (sometimes running downhill can be just as hard, and as likely to give one a stitch!) So how can we live out the Christian faith like an athlete?

> The *gymnasium* was characteristic of the Greek world and the baths of the Roman world, but in New Testament times hybrid or combination structures developed so that the gymnasia had swimming pools and the baths had exercise facilities. Since athletes were especially seen as under the patronage of Hermes and Hercules, statues and altars to them were normally present. Each city had exercise facilities. At Ephesus there are the extensive ruins of the Harbour Bath Gymnasium built under Domitian at the time St John wrote Revelation. The most impressive complex is at Sardis. It was built later than New Testament times and covers an area of 5.5 acres. Athletic contests took place in the *stadion.* Ephesus, like other cities, had a major stadium and regular contests.

The farmer (2 Timothy 2:6) The farmer, in an age when virtually everything had to done by hand, had to work hard all through the year. Farming involved physical labour to the point of exhaustion. It meant working all hours when bringing in the harvest or when an animal was ill or giving birth. Once more Paul is stressing that we cannot be a half-hearted part-time Christian. Commitment is needed, and without it there is no worthwhile harvest. Jesus called his first disciples to be fishers of men and referred to the harvest as those who needed to be told the good news and so have the opportunity to become Christians. Paul certainly realised how vital it was to pass on the good news to others. This famous prayer was certainly true for him: to give and not to count the cost, to fight and not to heed the wounds, to toil and not to seek for rest, to labour and to ask for no reward except the joy of doing God's will. How far does that describe us?

The road builder (2 Timothy 2:15) This picture is hidden in the English translation of the Greek *orthotomein*. The word was used in Paul's day to refer to a road builder who cut a straight road, or a mason who cut and squared a stone so that it fitted perfectly into the building. The Romans were famous for their road building and many of their roads can be seen today. Ephesus still has roads that Paul walked along—fine marble roads laid on strong foundations. Likewise after 2,000 years there are many fine buildings still standing because the stone masons cut a precise fit. Sophocles used this Greek word to describe someone giving good clear teaching. Our correct handling of the Bible and Christian teaching does involve careful study so that we know what the teaching meant to those who first heard it and then how it applies to life today.

(C)
Letters to the seven churches of Revelation

Patmos

Patmos is a small island measuring about 10 miles long by up to 5 miles wide about 60 miles south-west of Ephesus. There is a small harbour on the east coast in the lee of its hills which has provided an anchorage down the centuries. It was ceded by Turkey to Greece at the end of the second world war. Pliny, a Roman historian, tells us that in John's day it was used as a prison. Prisoners may have been employed in the mines. Locals claim a cave to be the place where John received his vision. There is also an important Greek Orthodox seminary and monastery.

John wrote this book which we call Revelation, in the form of an apocalypse. An apocalypse means an unveiling or revealing of anything that has been kept secret or concealed. If we read on through the book of Revelation we find it is full of strange, even bizarre images. There are strange beasts, one even having ten horns and seven heads. There is plenty of smoke, fire, lightning, thunder, hail and blood. The number seven is not only linked to the churches we will visit but also to seven stars (2:1), seven lampstands (2:1), seven seals (5:1), seven trumpets (8:2), seven angels with seven plagues (15:1), seven bowls of wrath (16:1), and a woman with seven heads (17:3). In Jewish thought the number seven stands for completeness or perfection. The concept comes from the seven 'days' in creation and this leads on to a seven-day week.

The overall message of the book of Revelation is that God reigns. At present his almighty power and authority are hidden but one day all will be revealed and all people will realize that God is King of kings and Lord of lords. In Handel's *Messiah*, both the 'Hallelujah chorus' and 'Worthy is the Lamb that was slain' seek to sum up in music the whole ethos of this letter of John to the churches.

> 'God is in control, no matter how things may look. Christ, not the emperor, is the Lord of history. He has the key of destiny itself. And he is coming again to execute justice. There is a glorious, wonderful future for every faithful believer ... and it is in God's hands. His love and care for his people is unfailing ... The book is firmly rooted in history, proclaiming Christ the Lord of history.'
>
> *(Lion Handbook to the Bible*, p.645)

Images like the ten-horned beast are obviously to be taken figuratively. So how do we approach the letters to the churches in Revelation 2-3? Scholars are agreed that John is writing to seven actual churches, just as when Paul wrote to the churches in Corinth and elsewhere. They suggest that we use the same principle as in other New Testament letters, that although the messages were primarily for the named churches, they also relate to us as members of Christ's church today.

But what about all those strange images? How do we interpret those which come in the letters to the seven churches? If we are not to take the images in the rest of the book in any historical or literal way, would this not also apply to the images in Revelation chapters 2-3?

There is good reason to take the messages to the churches in a different way from the rest of the book. We are told that these are letters to specific churches that the remainder of the book is a revelation of what is happening in heaven. We may not have the words to describe heaven but we certainly have the words to describe the church on earth.

Given that Christ is speaking to real churches, we still have some problems in interpreting the symbolic language employed. So here are some guidelines I have adopted:

a) The letters were written during the reign of the Emperor Domitian (AD81-96). Domitian was the younger son of the Emperor Vespasian and he was a megalomaniac. The Emperor Caligula (AD37-41) had claimed to be a god in human form but historians of his day are united in saying that he was insane. All the evidence about Domitian suggests that he was of a sound mind. Yet he decreed that throughout the empire every official document should begin 'Our Lord and our God Domitian commands'. It was an act of treason if one refused to call him god. Christians acknowledge only one God. Under Domitian many suffered for their faith, and this was the reason why John was in prison. The shadow of Domitian, therefore, hangs over the letters.

b) I am assuming that the vast majority of Christians in these churches were not Jews and would interpret images like a pillar in the temple as a tradition in their own city, rather than as a reference to the situation in the Holy Land. In most of the letters there is a clear reference to the Old Testament. Balaam (Numbers 25), Jezebel (2 Kings 19), David and Jerusalem all receive a mention and Psalm 2:9 is quoted. However, unless the link to the Old Testament is obvious I will interpret the messages as making use of local knowledge to which all members could relate.

John writes to seven churches

A letter to Ephesus

Revelation 2:1-7

1 To the angel of the church in Ephesus write: 'These are the words of him who holds the seven stars in his right hand and walks among the seven golden lampstands:

2 I know your deeds, your hard work and your perseverance. I know that you cannot tolerate wicked men, that you have tested those who claim to be apostles but are not, and have found them false.

3 You have persevered and have endured hardships for my name, and have not grown weary.

4 Yet I hold this against you: You have forsaken your first love.

5 Remember the height from which you have fallen! Repent and do the things you did at first. If you do not repent, I will come to you and remove your lampstand from its place.

6 But you have this in your favour: You hate the practices of Nicolaitans, which I also hate.

7 He who has an ear, let him hear what the Spirit says to the churches. To him who overcomes, I will give the right to eat from the tree of life, which is in the paradise of God.'

Notes - please also read
What Christ Thinks of the Church by John Stott, p.16f.
The Church under Fire by Stephen Travis, p.27f.

Introduction
To the angel of the church—either the guardian angel or the messenger (same word in Greek) who would read the letter.

Description of God

Who holds the seven stars (v.1). The seven churches are held in Christ's hand - held or enclosed in the grip of his hand as we would hold a table tennis ball and not as we would hold a football. 'When Domitian's young son died in AD83, he proclaimed him to be a god, and coins were struck showing ... the child ... playing with the stars' (Travis, p.30). The churches totally belong to God. *He walks among.* Christ is present and active among them. He is there, rather than looking down from above. *Lampstands*—the location of the church. Ephesus was the leading church of the area so the seven churches are spoken to as one group. The greater the church, the greater would be its fall.

Description of the Church

Hard work (v.2)—exhausting labour; the church was a hive of activity, but did they work for the right motive? *Perseverance*—constancy under trial, sticking to it through thick and thin. Orthodoxy - John's Epistles were written to Ephesus and give ways of testing who are true believers. As Ephesus was an important trade centre, it was visited by many Christians. Ignatius wrote to them soon after this time, pointing out: 'You all live according to truth, and no heresy has a home among you; indeed, you do not so much as listen to anyone if they speak of anything except Jesus Christ in truth.'

Fault of the Church

Forsaken your first love (v.4). Paul had begun the church in Ephesus forty years earlier. While in Ephesus, he had written to the church in Corinth. Part of that letter is the famous passage on love, 1 Corinthians 13, in which Paul, as Jesus had done with the two key commandments, puts love above all other Christian attributes. Later Paul had written to them, *I pray that you , being rooted and established in love, may have power ... to grasp how wide and long, and high and deep is the love of Christ, and to know this love that surpasses knowledge* (Eph.3:17-19). The first generation of Christians was dying out. The next generation was not so keen. The church had become more settled, more inward-looking, lacking in enthusiasm. Worship for them was more of a duty than a joy. John, in his epistles which were probably written to the Ephesians, constantly stresses that love is the key: e.g. *Dear children, let us not love with words or tongue but with actions and in truth* (1 John 3:18). John as a very old man seems to have had but one message: 'Love one another'.

Command to the Church
Repent and do the things you did at first (v.5). How easy it is for the first flush of enthusiasm to wear off. The Christians needed a change of mind that would lead to a change of behaviour. The word 'repent' comes from the military command 'about turn'. To repent is to turn to Christ and look to him for direction. If something is wrong in our lives the best way is to deal with it as quickly as possible rather than wait until others force us to change.

Warning of Judgement
Christ will *remove* its *lampstand*. The Ephesians thought of themselves as the light of Asia. Soon the town and the church were to lose that role. There are two possible meanings a) that he would blot out their existence by removing his presence (a church that has ceased to shine has lost its reason for existence) or b) that they would be removed to a new site. The old town, and with it the old church, would be broken down. This actually happened a few years after John wrote down this message. John Stott comments, 'The church has no light without love. Only when its love burns can its light shine' (p.27).

Message to the Faithful
Paul had warned the Ephesian elders at Miletus to look out for false teachers and they had taken this up. *Hate the Nicolaitans* (v.6). These may have been followers of Nicolas of Antioch (Acts 6:5), whom tradition says rejected the decrees of Acts 15 and saw no wrong in Christians eating meat that had been sacrificed to idols. If so, Balaamites of Pergamum would have taught in a similar vein. Their basic teaching was that, as we are saved by faith alone, Christ has set us free from the law. Irenaeus said 'they lived lives of unrestrained indulgence' and Clement said 'they abandoned themselves to pleasure like goats'. They taught that Christians can take part in all the immoral behaviour of the heathen around us. Christian liberty had become Christian licence. It is hard to be certain to whom John is referring. The word *Nikolaos* means in Greek 'the destroyer of my people', so this could have been another group. We can be certain that they were a sect that was causing much harm to the church.

Promise to the Church
To eat from the tree of life, which is in the paradise of God (v.7). Paradise is a Persian word and was used there to describe the garden of the king where trees were

a prominent feature, as they are in the gardens of our stately homes. The word 'paradise' was adopted throughout the ancient world as a picture of heaven. So Jesus promised the dying thief that he would be with him in paradise. For Jews and Christians it was like Eden restored. The garden of Eden had a tree of life (Gen. 3:22) and a tree of life was also found in the temple of Artemis. It was a date tree and symbolized the fertility of nature. Christians knew that this tree could never give true life. Only God could do that. He alone possessed the tree of life. The tree which gave immortality was not in the Temple of Artemis but in heaven (Rev. 22:2,14,19). It was a promise of eternal life.

Exhortation to Hear

This comes in all the letters. Those who had spiritual understanding were to read and apply the letters. Compare Christ's statement at the end of the parable of the sower (Matt. 13:9)—*He who has ears, let him hear*. Also 1 Corinthians 2:10-16, the things of God can only be understood by those who are born again by the Spirit.

A letter to Smyrna

Revelation 2:8-11

> 8 To the angel of the church in Smyrna write: 'These are the words of him who is the First and the Last, who died and came to life again.
> 9 I know your afflictions and your poverty - yet you are rich! I know the slander of those who say they are Jews and are not, but are a synagogue of Satan.
> 10 Do not be afraid of what you are about to suffer. I tell you, the devil will put some of you in prison to test you, and you will suffer persecution for ten days. Be faithful, even to the point of death, and I will give you the crown of life.
> 11 He who has an ear, let him hear what the Spirit says to the churches. He who overcomes will not be hurt at all by the second death'.

Notes - please also read

What Christ Thinks of the Church by John Stott, p.28f.
The Church under Fire by Stephen Travis, p.43f.

Description of God

The First and the Last (v.8). In Revelation 1:8 Christ is described as the Alpha and Omega - the first and last letters of the Greek alphabet. God was there at the big bang, or whatever started material creation, and will be there at the end of the universe. He is above and outside the limits of space and time as we experience them. *Died and came to life*—that was true for Christ when he died on Good Friday and lived again on the third day (1 Thess. 4:14; 1 Cor. 15:20). Clement remarked that Jesus turned all our sunsets into a sunrise. He had changed a guess into knowledge and a probability into a certainty. Although attempts have been made to find the place where Jesus lay in the tomb, and the Garden tomb in Jerusalem is a useful site to contemplate that event, the key message is that of the angels: 'He is not here, he has risen'. For Christians in Smyrna, death was a daily threat, but they knew Christ conquers death. Their city Smyrna had a history of dying and then suddenly re-emerging as a powerful metropolis.

Description of the Church

Afflictions (v.9) (*thlipsis*) pressure. Today if we make our stand as a Christian and are known to attend church and the Christian Union we can come under pressure at work, in the home, and at school. Yet whatever our circumstances, opposition, or worry, Christ knows what we are going through and will give us power to overcome. The writer to the Hebrews put it this way: 'Let us fix our eyes on Jesus, the author and perfecter of our faith, who for the joy set before him endured the cross, scorning its shame, and sat down at the right hand of the throne of God. Consider him who endured such opposition from sinful men, so that you will not grow weary and lose heart' (Heb. 12:2-3).

Poverty—destitute—they had nothing materially. Perhaps they had been thrown out of their jobs, or Jews and others were boycotting their businesses. If your aim is to get rich quick, then honesty is by no means the best policy. Living by Christian standards sometimes carries with it hardship. But they had God. They were rich in things that mattered (1 Cor. 1:26; James 2:5). Christ tells us to think of the future (Matt. 6:20; 19:21; Luke 12:21). Poverty existed then just as much as always. There were numerous slaves. Pliny mentions in disgust that a bride wearing a dress worth £500,000 was riding past people who were starving. The world has not changed!

Slander The Jews were exempt from such acts as sacrifice to the emperor. In the early days the church was regarded as a Jewish sect, but the Jews made a point of dissociating themselves from Christians and reporting them to the authorities. The Jews had a voice in high places: e.g. Nero was influenced by Poppaea (empress) and Alitarus (actor) who were both Jewish proselytes. Christ calls the Jews the synagogue of Satan. Wesley once said to a similar group in the Christian church, 'Your God is my devil' (cf. Acts 13:50; 14:2,5,19; 17:5; 24:2). Forty years after this letter Polycarp suffered martyrdom rather than sacrifice to the emperor. Some commentators claim that the *mark of the beast* (Rev. 13:7) was the mark given to someone who had sacrificed to the emperor. In John's day the Jews of Smyrna were opposing the Christians because a number of the Jewish community had become Christians. Hostility is often intense when communities feel threatened by such changes of allegiance. Sadly they turned from being the Lord's synagogue into that of Satan, the accuser of God's people. However, it is important to note that the first Christians were Jews, that John who wrote these words was a Jew, and there were Jewish Christians who were among those who received this letter.

Command to the Church

Do not be afraid ... the devil will put some of you in prison (v.10). In Roman times prison was often the preliminary to execution—there were no long-term prisoners. *ten days* a short time before execution; the length of the games in Smyrna, during which they might be set against the gladiators or wild beasts, or before the hue and cry would die down and they would be released. *Faithful even to the point of death*—Smyrna had always been faithful to Rome. It had one of the first temples dedicated to emperor-worship and had always sought to be regarded as the principle city in the area for that cult. Now Christians must show their faithfulness to Christ even if it involves death. Jesus offered his disciples three things: constant trouble, power to be completely fearless, and absurd happiness (e.g. Matt. 5:11-12; 10:17-36). 'The whole story of God's dealings with the world is cross shaped' (Travis). 'In the age-long battle between God and Satan, God knows no other victory and needs no other victory that that which is won by the cross of Christ, faithfully proclaimed to the world by the martyr witness of his church' (G B Caird).

Promise to the Church

Crown of Life (stephanos) four possible interpretations:

a) given after a victory in the games, for a Christian runs a race (1 Cor. 9:24f.).

b) worn at festivals, or by a bride and bridegroom at a wedding—a life of joy.

c) presented for loyal service—a laurel crown worn by magistrates, officials etc. Christ gives us a crown for loyalty.

d) the crown of Smyrna—Mt Pagos and its fine buildings overlooked the city as does the fortress today. Locals called it the crown because of the ring of fine white mansions circling the hill.

Second death (v.11). Jewish rabbis regarded this as the total extinction of the utterly wicked. To worship Caesar may save a man here but it will be of no help in the future (Matt. 10:28).

Paul, writing to Timothy, quoted a well known Christian hymn:

> If we died with him, we will also live with him;
> if we endure; we will also reign with him;
> if we disown him, he will also disown us.

For the Christians in Smyrna that was a motto to see them through the difficult days that lay ahead.

Footnote
The letter to Smyrna is the only one that contains no note of blame. It is the only one of the seven cities where the church has continued down the centuries. Today Izmir is the third largest city in Turkey and has several churches. Christ encourages them to face the hard future trusting in him.

A letter to Pergamum

Revelation 2:12-17
12 To the angel of the church in Pergamum write: 'These are the words of him who has the sharp, double-edged sword.
13 I know where you live—where Satan has his throne. Yet you remain true to my name. You did not renounce your faith in me, even in the days of Antipas, my faithful witness, who was put to death in your city—where Satan lives.
14 Nevertheless, I have a few things against you: You have

people there who hold to the teaching of Balaam, who taught Balak to entice the Israelites to sin by eating food sacrificed to idols and by committing sexual immorality.

15 Likewise you also have those who hold to the teaching of the Nicolaitans.

16 Repent therefore! Otherwise, I will soon come to you and will fight against them with the sword of my mouth.

17 He who has an ear, let him hear what the Spirit says to the churches. To him who overcomes, I will give some of the hidden manna. I will also give him a white stone with a new name written on it, known only to him who receives it'.

Notes - please also read
What Christ Thinks of the Church by John Stott, p.41f.
The Church under Fire by Stephen Travis, p.59f.

Description of God
The sharp double-edged sword (v.12). The sword is of the type used by the Roman governor. The pro-consul was invested with the right of the sword, i.e. the power to order the death penalty. The consul thought he possessed such power but in reality this belongs to God. Ephesians 6:17 likens the Word of God to a sword. The short two-edged sword looked like a tongue. God's Word too has the power of life—to those who accept it, and death—to those who reject. See also Revelation 1:16; 19:11f. and Hebrews. 4:11.

Description of the Church
I know where you live—where Satan has his throne (v.13). Satan's throne could have been the major temple of Asklepios, the god who used snakes, a biblical symbol for Satan, as part of the healing process. The snake badge of Asklepios is still used today in some medical badges.

Another possible interpretation for the *throne* is that Pergamum was the capital of Roman Asia, so the emperor had his local throne here and Christians were under constant threat. 'Conscientious refusal to take part in worship of the emperor could be interpreted as treason by a regime, like Domitian's, intent on suppressing dangerous ideas' (Travis, p. 60).

However, most commentators suggest that Satan's throne was the huge temple of Zeus that dominated the lower town.

Whatever it is that is being alluded to here, Christ knows that they dwell where Satan's seat is. Satan not only exists in Pergamum but he appears to reign supreme. Here Satan is at his most powerful and authoritative. His realm is where darkness and error have gained a grip. The light of Christ is dimmed. It is here that the Christians live and are to go on living. Here at Satan's throne they must witness. There is no question of leaving for easier towns (cp. Mark 5—the man of Gerasa; 1 Cor. 7:12f.). There had been an outbreak of persecution but the Christians had held fast. Antipas had been martyred—*my faithful witness*. To be all out for Christ often means that we have to suffer. We have to take up our cross daily. But to suffer for him also means that we will reign with him. In Revelation 1:5 Christ is called a faithful witness or martyr—it is the same Greek word. In such circumstances it is encouraging to know that Christ is fully aware of our situation. He is present among us. His Spirit is able to give us strength.

You remain true to my name. In the Bible the 'name' is a way of expressing all that is known about a person. In the same way today, when a name is mentioned we do not think about the individual letters, (e.g. PETER) but about a person we know called by that name. *You did not renounce your faith in me*—'Truth must move from the place where it simply grips our minds to the place where it grips our lives as well' (I Barclay).

Fault of the Church
Balaamites or Nicolaitans—cp. notes on Ephesus and Thyatira. In Numbers 25:1 and 31:16 the Israelites had taken part in heathen practices. They had been influenced through Balaam by the Midianites they had conquered, to eat pagan food and take pagan women (Num. 31:16). Once again compromise was creeping into the church. Social parties where God's name was neither loved nor respected had proved too great a temptation. Immorality had crept in: cp. 1 Corinthians 5, and Romans 1. Relationships outside marriage were regarded as the norm. It was a distinctive part of Christianity to lay down faithfulness in these matters. Such standards of faithfulness in marriage even surprised Christ's disciples (Matt. 19:10; Stott p.45).

Command to the Church

Repent: no half-way house. Something more was needed than keeping a look-out for evil. They needed to get rid of evil in whatever form it appeared among them.

Warning of Judgement

I will soon come to you and fight ... with the sword of my mouth (v.16). Destruction will be rapid and sudden. When God speaks it is not just in words; he has the power to execute them. God spoke and it was done (Gen. 1). Balaam was killed by a sword (Num. 31:8). To sin is bad, but to condone sin or to teach others is very serious (Matt. 18: 6). How strong should church discipline be today?

Promise to the Church

To him who overcomes (v.17). To those who come out of worldly compromise, two things are promised. *Manna* Exodus 16:4f—bread from heaven. The people didn't know what it was, so they said *What is it?* (in Hebrew *manna;* Exod. 16:15) and kept asking the question for forty years! Psalm 78:24-25 describes it as angels' food. The rabbis said manna would return in the messianic age. The Christians who had to give up the earthly pleasures of parties etc. would receive heavenly food. John 6,33f. tells us that the true bread of life is Christ, and Christians will feed upon him in all his glory.

A white stone with a new name written on it, known only to him who receives it. Suggestions as to what this is are numerous:

a) white stones were used by juries for acquittal: black for condemnation. A white stone was also inscribed SP and given by the people to a gladiator who was then allowed to retire and not have to face again the possibility of death in the arena.

b) A white stone with a code name on it was a ticket for the state lottery.

c) Revelation 3:4; 6:2—white equals holiness. Therefore the stone represents a clean heart, but what is the secret new name? It ought not to be the new character, which should be obvious. Maybe it is a special name given by Christ as a sign of his love, just as couples sometimes use names of endearment.

d) A precious pellucid diamond inscribed with Christ's name. So the believer receives Christ in glory.

e) Jewels of the heathen often had a god's name inscribed on them. Christ too will give Christians a token, an assurance of salvation—his name engraved upon their hearts (Rev. 3:12; 14:1; 22:4).

A letter to Thyatira

Revelation 2:18-29

18 To the angel of the church in Thyatira write: 'These are the words of the Son of God, whose eyes are like blazing fire and whose feet are like burnished bronze.

19 I know your deeds, your love and faith, your service and perseverance, and that you are now doing more than you did at first.

20 Nevertheless, I have this against you: You tolerate that woman Jezebel, who calls herself a prophetess. By her teaching she misleads my servants into sexual immorality and the eating of food sacrificed to idols.

21 I have given her time to repent of her immorality, but she is unwilling.

22 So I will cast her on a bed of suffering, and I will make those who commit adultery with her suffer intensely, unless they repent of her ways.

23 I will strike her children dead. Then all the churches will know that I am he who searches hearts and minds, and I will repay each of you according to your deeds.

24 Now I say to the rest of you in Thyatira, to you who do not hold to her teaching and have not learned Satan's so-called deep secrets (I will not impose any other burden on you):

25 Only hold on to what you have until I come.

26 To him who overcomes and does my will to the end, I will give authority over the nations—

27 "He will rule them with an iron sceptre; he will dash them to pieces like pottery" - just as I have received authority from my Father.

28 I will also give him the morning star.

29 He who has an ear, let him hear what the Spirit says to the churches.'

Notes – please also read
What Christ Thinks of the Church by John Stott, p.58f.
The Church under Fire by Stephen Travis, p.75f.

Description of God
It is clear from the beginning of the letter that this is not going to be an easy message for the church. *Eyes like blazing fire* (v.18), i.e. able to hunt out and deal with corruption. Here are eyes blazing with anger against sin and with a penetrating gaze able to see deep into every church member. Fire burns up dross (1Cor. 3:13f.). *Feet like burnished bronze*—power to crush opposition and find the good among the bad. Bronze hoofs are put on the oxen when they are treading out the grain—this is still done today and is a common sight in a farming area. They were made at Thyatira. 'The word for burnished bronze occurs only here in Greek literature, and John uses it because it has special associations for his readers. The coppersmiths of Thyatira had developed a sophisticated technique for making a particularly fine kind of brass, and alloy of copper and zinc ... its manufacture was a secret closely guarded by the coppersmiths' guild. (Travis, p.77).

Description of the Church
I know your deeds, your love and faith, your service and perseverance (v.19). Jesus is the *kardiognostes* (heart-knower). Nothing is concealed from him, good or bad. The letter is to be one of warning and criticism but it begins with praise. Real criticism should encourage and not discourage. Jezebel's group in the church might be getting all the attention but Jesus knows those Christians who, although they might be at work in the background, are those who really count. They have the motivating force of love and faith and combine them with service and perseverance. 'Thyatira understood that the Christian life is a life of growth, of progress, of development. Ephesus was backsliding; Thyatira was moving forward. The church of Ephesus had abandoned the love it had at first; the church of Thyatira was exceeding the works it did at first' (Stott, p.59).

The Fault of the Church

The Christians were being led astray by Jezebel to join in the trade guilds that seemed to have dominated life in this city (v.20). Jezebel is most likely a false name. She is likened to the wife of King Ahab, who led Israel into sin at the time of Elijah (1Kings 17f.). She may have been the wife of one of the church leaders just as Jezebel of old was the wife of the king. Anyway, she held a high position as a prophetess (allowed to preach). Her arguments seem to have been a) you should know about the evil of the world; b) your material prosperity depends on your being in the union and Christians should set a good example by being good prosperous citizens. 'At Pergamum some Christians' *lives* were threatened by the emperor-cult. At Thyatira their *livelihood* is threatened by the trade-guilds. And perhaps it is easier to recognize and resist the pressure of a political regime than the pressure that comes from social and economic forces' (Travis, p.76).

Christ's reply, which has always been the church's position was a) Don't dabble with evil; b) God, not material prosperity, should come first. Living by Christian principles may not be commercially advantageous. The church from the start was convinced that there should be no compromise with idolatry (Acts 15 etc.). In every age Christians are called to live **in** the world without becoming **of** the world. Does the same problem exist today, e.g. tax dodging, certain jobs, and some social events, societies and clubs? Notice that the threat of annihilation did not come from outside the church but from inside. The state did not have to interfere as at Smyrna and Pergamum. The church in its desire for wealth and social friendship was destroying itself.

Command to the Church

The opportunity to repent has gone unheeded (v.20).

Warning of Judgement

Tribulation physical and spiritual (v.22). There is no escape because God searches out the mind (cf. v.18).

Message to the Faithful

Hold on to what you have (v.24). No further burden—only hold fast.

Promise to the Church

Authority over the nations (v.26). Poor weak Thyatira had never ruled over anyone, let alone the nations. Sir William Ramsey points out that the whole situation of the town gives an impression of 'weakness, subjection and dependence.' It was a garrison town, the first line of defence that was expected to fall easily to any invader. Yet their rule will be like earthen pots trying to resist an iron rod. The large pottery jars of the ancient world that were used to store water and oil were a vulnerable object for destruction when armies invaded cities like Thyatira. The people of Thyatira then, as now, had a flourishing pottery industry. They needed it to replace pots so frequently shattered by invaders. Now the iron rod of Christ's victory could be in their hands.

Verses 26-27 are a reference to Psalm 2. This psalm refers to the triumphant work of God through his conquering Messiah. 'It is an amazing act of faith that the little Christian church, which was under attack by the vast Roman Empire, should take that promise and appropriate it to itself. From every human point of view the only thing which could possibly await the church was total destruction and annihilation; but from the divine point of view the thing which awaits the church is total triumph' (W Barclay).

The morning star (v.28; cf.Rev.22:16)—Christ is symbolically the morning star. Just before dawn, the planet Venus shines out as it reflects the sun's light. But the one who rules the heavens is Christ, not the planets or stars, or the emperor who claimed to be descended from Venus. So true believers will reign in splendour in the power of the resurrection. They too will receive power just as Christ received power from his Father. If we follow Christ faithfully we, too, will reign with him, and we will enjoy his presence now and for ever.

A letter to Sardis

Revelation 3:1-6

1 To the angel of the church in Sardis write: 'These are the words of him who holds the seven spirits of God and the seven stars. I know your deeds; you have a reputation of being alive, but you are dead.
2 Wake up! Strengthen what remains and is about to die, for I have not found your deeds complete in the sight of my God.

3 Remember, therefore, what you have received and heard; obey it, and repent. But if you do not wake up, I will come like a thief, and you will not know at what time I will come to you.

4 Yet you have a few people in Sardis who have not soiled their clothes. They will walk with me, dressed in white, for they are worthy.

5 He who overcomes will, like them, be dressed in white. I will never blot out his name from the book of life, but will acknowledge his name before my Father and his angels.

6 He who has an ear, let him hear what the Spirit says to the churches.'

Notes – please also read

What Christ Thinks of the Church by John Stott, p.74f.
The Church under Fire by Stephen Travis, p.87f.

Description of God

Seven spirits (v.1). The letters to the churches begin with this description (1:4). The holy all-sidedness of Christ is opposed to the false all-sidedness of a sham Christianity. Christ offers the fullness of his Holy Spirit and of his light (seven stands for completeness) to those who are on the point of spiritual death. 'To his people, sunken in spiritual darkness and torpor, the lamp of faith waning and almost extinguished in their hearts, the Lord presents himself as able to revive, able to recover, able to bring back from the gates of spiritual death those who ask him' (R C Trench).

Description of the Church

'It is intriguing to note that Christ saw no infringement of the moral law, no immorality or association with semi-Christian sects such as the Balaamites and Nicolaitans. There was no Jezebel. Equally there appears to have been no pressure from outside; the Jews were not inciting the authorities to persecute the believers' (I Barclay).

A reputation of being alive, but you are dead. It enjoyed a reputation that it did not deserve. The church enjoyed peace but it was the peace of a cemetery. Why had this happened? Four reasons: a) the material and secular were predominant rather than the spiritual; b) they worshipped the glorious past, living on the memories of the former days and the way the church was run in their fathers' day; c) they were more concerned with forms than with life, more concerned with how things were done (ritual) than why they were done; d) they were more concerned with rules and systems than they were with Christ. There were those within the church who had *soiled their clothes* (v.4). We do not know the form this sin took. It was not high profile like that in Pergamum or Thyatira but it had a deadening effect just the same.

'The correct word for this behaviour is "hypocrisy". Originally the *hupokrites* was an actor, who plays a part on the stage. But the word came to be applied to any charlatan or pretender who assumes a role. Hypocrisy is make-believe; it is the "let's pretend" of religion' (Stott, p.81).

There are many examples in the Old Testament of dead religion. The prophets reminded the people that a pure heart was far more important than sacrifices. God required those who loved doing his will. Jesus likewise pointed out that many of the religious people of his day were like whitewashed tombs. They looked impressive but signified death. The outer facade of the church in Sardis hid the decaying structure behind. How long would it be before it all fell down?

Command to the Church
Christ's remedy is contained in five imperatives or commands.

a) *Strengthen* (v.2). To know yourself was the first law in Greek life, to strengthen the strong as well as the weak points. To neglect any area could lead to tragedy.

b) *our deeds*—Montgomery said 'One man can lose me a battle'. That happened twice at Sardis when individual soldiers, thinking their fortress was secure, opened the way for its destruction.

c) *Remember* (v.3).—do so constantly (present imperative), *what you have received* (perfect)—had and still have—a trust or deposit. 'They had received more than the gospel. They had received the Holy Spirit ... indeed the greatest gift the Christian has ever received. He enters our human personality and changes us from within. He fills us with love, joy and peace' (Stott, p. 86).

d) *Heard*—teaching about Christ they had received through Paul and others.

e) *Obey it and repent*—what is required is a clear-cut decision. The philosopher Epictetus, who lived at the time, used to denounce those who came to stare at him as if he was a statue and then do nothing about his teaching. Many did that to Jesus. In the Sermon on the Mount he points out that *everyone who hears these words of mine and puts them into practice is like a wise man who built his house on the rock* (Matt. 7:24).

Warning of Judgement

But if you do not wake up, I will come like a thief in the night. This reminds us of Christ's warnings about being ready (Matthew 24:43 refers to a thief in the night). It would remind those at Sardis of their own history, of the times when the town had been defeated and of the earthquake. It would also remind them of their present situation. Sardis was a has-been! It had been the capital of a mighty empire. It had been very wealthy, even creating the first coins. But it was in terminal decline. They had not even finished the temple to their city god.

Promise to the Church

A few were faithful. In the other churches a few had gone astray: here in Sardis it is only a few who remain faithful. To *those who have not soiled their clothes* (v.4). In the heathen religion of the time it was regarded as sacrilege to approach a god in soiled garments and this practice spread to the church (clean white surplices!). God promises blessing to the pure in heart. White garments were worn by a victor and the crowd which lined his route, and used to be worn by Christians at funerals to show that death was conquered by Christ (Isa. 61:10; Rev. 19:8). The white robes signified purity, festivity and victory. *They will walk with me, dressed in white, for they are worthy.* White robes were normal dress in these times. It was also common for close friends to be seen walking together, and it was a great privilege to be invited to walk with the king or emperor in his garden. The Bible begins with God walking with the first human pair in the garden. To those who wake up and repent, Eden is restored. The people of God in heaven are always described as wearing white (Rev. 6:11; 7:9f.).

Book of life (v.5). is mentioned in the Old Testament (Exo.32:32; Psa. 69:28; Mal. 3:16; Dan. 12:1; Psa. 139:16). The book of life in Sardis and other cites was the register of the living citizens (list of electors). Names were erased at death. While there is life there is hope. Spiritual victors will never be erased. *Acknowledge his name* (Matt. 10:32; Luke 12:8). Christ will acknowledge us but we must also we willing to acknowledge him. In the Anglican baptism service we say of the candidate, 'Do not be ashamed to confess the faith of Christ crucified. Fight valiantly under the banner of Christ against sin, the world, and the devil, and continue his faithful soldier and servant to the end of your life.' May that be true for us as for the faithful church members at Sardis.

Footnote
The church in Sardis survived for some time and the remains of churches from the first few centuries are proof of this. In the second century Bishop Melito of Sardis was one of the earliest Christians to make a pilgrimage to the Holy Land. He also wrote to the emperor arguing that the state had no valid reason to persecute Christians. So not all was lost.

A letter to Philadelphia

Revelation 3:7-13
7 To the angel of the church in Philadelphia write: 'These are the words of him who is holy and true, who holds the key of David. What he opens no-one can shut, and what he shuts no-one can open.

8 I know your deeds. See, I have placed before you an open door that no-one can shut. I know that you have little strength, yet you have kept my word and have not denied my name.

9 I will make those who are of the synagogue of Satan, who claim to be Jews though they are not, but are liars - I will make them come and fall down at your feet and acknowledge that I have loved you.

10 Since you have kept my command to endure patiently, I will also keep you from the hour of trial that is going to come upon the whole world to test those who live on the earth.

11 I am coming soon. Hold on to what you have, so that no-one will take your crown.

12 Him who overcomes I will make a pillar in the temple of my God. Never again will he leave it. I will write on him

the name of my God and the name of the city of my God, the new Jerusalem, which is coming down out of heaven from my God; and I will also write on him my new name. 13 He who has an ear, let him hear what the Spirit says to the churches.'

Notes - please also read
What Christ Thinks of the Church by John Stott, p.94f.
The Church under Fire by Stephen Travis, p.103f.

Description of God
Christ is *holy and true* (v.7) as opposed to what is illusory and spurious. *Holy* is the title for God used throughout the Bible. We have the vivid picture of God in Isaiah 6 when the prophet receives that vision of a God so holy that he cries out 'I am ruined! For I am a man of unclean lips, and I live among a people of unclean lips, and my eyes have seen the King, the Lord Almighty'.

Christ is also the *true* one. He is totally reliable, totally trustworthy. His word is truth. This was in stark contrast to the Emperor Domitian, who had just 'issued a decree requiring half the vineyards to be cut down. Philadelphia's soil produced vines in abundance, but was not so suitable for corn. So Domitian's decree seemed to its citizens like the action of an enemy, and a particularly cynical enemy at that' (Travis, p.105).

Key of David is a quote from Isaiah 22:22 (cp. Matt. 16:19; 28:18; Rev. 5:5). In Isaiah 22 the king gave Eliakim, his faithful steward, a special key so that he could come to him whenever he wished. So Christ opens the way to God.

Description of the Church
I know your deeds. See I have placed before you an open door (v.8).

a) The door of opportunity to tell others—every Christian should be like this. Here is an opportunity to know Christ and to serve him (2 Cor. 2:12; Col. 4:3; Acts 14:27). He has handed us the keys to enable others to come to know and love him. After Peter's confession at Caesarea Philippi, Jesus promised him, *I will give you the keys of the kingdom*. Peter was to use those keys on the day of Pentecost and in the years ahead when he brought many people to God.

b) The door of prayer—Christ has opened up the way of access to God.

c) Jesus is the door, e.g. the shepherd lying across the door of the sheepfold. Those within his sheepfold are secure from the whims of the emperor or the attacks of the Jews.

d) Jews had excommunicated the Christians - Christ never shuts anyone out.

e) This is the most likely meaning, namely, that whatever the Jews might claim as being the only people of God, God himself had the key to his kingdom and with it the right to welcome in those whom he chose.

'The doors stand wide open still. Christ invites us first to go in through the door of salvation, and then to go out through the door of service' (Stott, p.110).

Kept my word and have not denied my name. Two essentials of the Christian life are obedience to Christ in action and faithfulness to him in witness. They are loyal to Christ, and Christ will be loyal to them (v.10) in a far greater way than they had been loyal him, or than those of their city had been loyal to their founder and benefactors.

Message to the Faithful

Fall down at your feet (v.9). Christians who were being severely punished looked to God to vindicate them. Many of the early Christians were Jews or those of other races who had become 'God-fearers'. Down the centuries the Jews had seen themselves as a people needing God to come and vindicate them. The early Christians naturally adopted such promises of vindication, like those in Isaiah 49:23 where the enemies of God's chosen people will 'bow down before them with their faces to the ground; they will lick the dust at their feet'. Jewish Christians like Paul saw their fellow unbelieving Jews as outside the will of God and longed for them to be saved. They also knew that God would vindicate his people. God had intervened before to redeem his people at the Exodus and when they were in Babylonian captivity, and he can do so again.

I will keep you from the hour of trial (v.10). Christ will help the Christian in times when the future looks bleak (Isa. 43:2; Mark 13:20). *Chariots of Fire* is the story of Eric Liddell, who refused to run in the 100 metres (1924 Olympics) because it was held on a Sunday. He later ran in the 400 metres and set up the world record (Travis, p.112). However, the *hour of trial is going to come upon the whole world*. It is not just a time limited to the church at Philadelphia or to specific instances in our own generation. This trial will be universal in its scope. The Bible predicts such a time before Christ returns in power and glory. Yet there will also come a time when, as C S Lewis puts it, 'the author will walk on the stage and the play will be over'. God has placed a limit on such trials just as he put a limit on Job's sufferings.

Let no one take your crown (v.11). A crown was given to a victorious athlete at a festival, but here more likely the crown is given for loyal service—see comment on Smyrna.

Pillar in the temple of my God (v.12). It was a custom to erect a pillar in memory of some benefactor or famous person (Psa. 27:4). There were plenty of pillars lying broken from the earthquake. Others had withstood such an onslaught, like the great pillars from Philadelphia's church still standing today. God promises his people a pillar that will not fall. Such a pillar can only be our heavenly reward. By comparison, any earthly fame is short-lived. However, we are called upon to be like those pillars that give strength and support to our brothers and sisters in Christ. Some people support the church, others want the church to support them. What type are we?

Never again will he leave it. Earthquakes often caused the residents of Philadelphia, as those of other cities in the area, to flee the city. At such times homes were destroyed and they had to live in tents. For those who overcome, a permanent home is waiting in heaven.

My new name—Coins minted in the name of the new king or queen show their authority. In some places coins of the old regime were destroyed and re-minted. Christians should have God's name stamped on them to show where their loyalty lies. It is the name of One whose reign will never end.

A letter to Laodicea

> ### Revelation 3:14-22
> 14 To the angel of the church in Laodicea write: 'These are the words of the Amen, the faithful and true witness, the ruler of God's creation.

15 I know your deeds, that you are neither cold nor hot. I wish you were either one or the other!

16 So, because you are lukewarm—neither hot nor cold—I am about to spit you out of my mouth.

17 You say, `I am rich; I have acquired wealth and do not need a thing.' But you do not realise that you are wretched, pitiful, poor, blind and naked.

18 I counsel you to buy from me gold refined in the fire, so that you can become rich; and white clothes to wear, so that you can cover your shameful nakedness; and salve to put on your eyes, so that you can see.

19 Those whom I love I rebuke and discipline. So be earnest, and repent.

20 Here I am! I stand at the door and knock. If anyone hears my voice and opens the door, I will come in and eat with him, and he with me.

21 To him who overcomes, I will give the right to sit with me on my throne, just as I overcame and sat down with my Father on his throne.

22 He who has an ear, let him hear what the Spirit says to the churches.'

Notes – please also read

What Christ Thinks of the Church by John Stott, p.111f.
The Church under Fire by Stephen Travis, p.117f.

Description of God

The Amen (v.14). Christ frequently put amen (verily, truly) before his statements to show that their truth was guaranteed. We use it to affirm our agreement with the prayer.

Ruler of creation (John 1:1-3; Col. 1:15f.; Rev. 21:6; 22:13). The Roman emperor claimed to be the ruler, the *princeps,* but compared with Christ his kingdom was very much of this temporary world.

Description of the Church

This is the one letter with no word of praise and no redeeming feature; a grim distinction that must have made this rich church wince.

Lukewarm (v.16). A reference to the main water supply which came from five miles to the south, but the water flowing down from Pamukkale may also have been used by those in the northern suburbs. Near the Phygian gate to the south there were some drinking fountains which contained water renowned for its high mineral content and lukewarm temperature. Unsuspecting visitors often ended up spitting it out in disgust. Christ says: If you were hot for bathing or cold for drinking you would be useful, but as it is, I feel towards you the way you feel toward your water supply—you make me vomit. Laodicean Christians had become of no real use. It is important to note that in this context both hot and cold are seen as good (v.15). It is not that *hot* is boiling with enthusiasm for God and *cold* is spiritually dead. Laodiceans and Christ valued the cold spring water as much as the water from the hot springs. The problem was their luke-warm, flabby, half-hearted deeds. 'What Jesus Christ desires and deserves is the reflection which leads to commitment and the commitment which is born of reflection. This is the meaning of wholeheartedness, of being aflame for God' (Stott, p.115).

Fault of the Church

They trusted in their wealth, clothing and health. They were rich and they knew it. It resulted in pride, defiance and conceit. This attitude is far too obvious in some situations today. God seems an optional extra, a useful add-on but not part of life's main programme.

Command to the Church

At most markets, traders seek to attract customers by calling out the good features or prices of their wares. That would certainly have been the case in the crowded streets of Laodicea. Christ urges his people to turn a deaf ear to those urging the purchase of local goods and to buy from him things of lasting worth. Lay up for yourselves treasure in heaven. Notice that they have to buy from Christ the very things citizens of Laodicea felt they had in plenty—gold, clothing, and eye-powder. John Stott writes, 'I can never read this verse without being strangely moved. He is the great God of the expanding universe. He has countless galaxies of stars at his fingertips. The heaven and the heaven of heavens cannot contain him. He is the creator and sustainer of all things, the Lord God Almighty. He has the right to issue orders for us to obey. He prefers to give advice which we need not heed. He could command; he chooses to counsel. He respects the freedom with which he has ennobled us'(Stott, p. 119). *Gold refined in the fire* (v.18). All that glisters is certainly not gold in the Turkish jewellery shops of today, and maybe that was true even in John's time. Certainly Christ urges the church to obtain from him pure gold (cf. 2 Cor. 8:9).

White clothes to wear. Sir W Ramsey points out that the local cloth was 'soft in texture and glossy black in colour.' The Bible always relates pure white with holiness, and without holiness we cannot enter the presence of God.

Salve to put on your eyes. This may have been a compound powder in line with the teaching of Herophilos of Laodicea, who taught that complex disorders needed compound mixtures; or it may have been the powder referred to by Galen as 'Phrygian stone'. Whatever it was, it was useless when compared with Christ's healing power. As Isaiah 55 points out, the gifts of God are free.

In verse 19, love is seen in concern. The best pupil or sportsman is always encouraged to aim for something higher, but such attainment will involve hard work. *Earnest*—the verb is in the present imperative and involves continuous action; *repent* is in the aorist—a definite act. So we can best translate 'make your decision to turn to God and then show your zeal for him throughout the rest of your life'.

Promise to the Church

I stand at the door and knock (v.20). Has the market trader even gone to the length of following his prospective customer home? Here is an offer of real fellowship. Similar words are used of a meal in the coming kingdom of Christ (Mark 13:29; John 5:9). Christ is not knocking at the door of the unbeliever but at the door of the church. Sadly it was the church which had left Christ outside, so would there be someone in its membership who would open the door to him? Notice that Christ has taken the initiative and is knocking at the door; no one has invited him to come. It is now up to some in the church to respond and let him in. Holman Hunt's picture in St Paul's Cathedral shows no handle on the outside of the door.

In their culture there were three meals each day: *akratisma* (breakfast) a slice of bread dipped in wine; *ariston* (lunch) a scratch meal often while still out; *deip-*

non (dinner/supper) a main meal where one sat and talked a long while. Christ offers to come to supper. This is not a courtesy call but a long stay.

Sit with me on my throne (v.21). In Revelation 22:1 we have a picture of the throne of God. The church which received the greatest condemnation is also offered the greatest glory, namely to reign with Christ in glory. To be seated was a symbolic way of stating that a task had been completed. The phrase comes from Psalm 110:1, *The Lord says to my Lord: 'Sit at my right hand until I make your enemies a footstool for your feet.'* Jesus promised his followers that they would reign with him in glory (Matt.19:28) and Paul points out that the saints will judge the world (1 Cor. 6:2).

In conclusion

Sir W Ramsey in *Letters to the Seven Churches* (p.432) makes the following observations on the churches as they were in the last century before the persecution of the Christians, and before modern development which has taken place in the last fifty years:

a) Two only are condemned absolutely and without pardon: Sardis is dead; Laodicea is rejected. Two only are at this present day absolutely deserted and uninhabited, Sardis and Laodicea.

b) Two churches only are praised in an unreserved, hearty, and loving way: Smyrna and Philadelphia. And two cities have enjoyed and earned the glory of being champions of Christianity in the centuries of war that ended in the Turkish conquest. The last two cities to yield long after all others had succumbed and which are still today important towns are Smyrna and Philadelphia.

c) Two other churches were treated with mingled praise and blame, though on the whole the praise outweighs the blame; for their faith, constant endurance, works, love, service and patience are heartily praised though they have become tainted with heresy. These are Pergamum and Thyatira, both of which are still small towns—Bergama and Akhisar.

d) One church will be moved from its place; and Ephesus was moved to a site three kilometres away. The modern town of Seljuk is by the new site.

The whole book of Revelation is written to these churches, replete with references to contemporaneous events and circumstances. Believers were being persecuted severely, bitterly. Their blood was being poured out. (Rev.1:9; 7:14; 6:10; 16:6; 17:6; 19:2). Some were pining away in dingy dungeons or were about to be imprisoned (2:10). They were suffering hunger, thirst, famine (6:8; 7:18). Some had been cast to wild beasts or beheaded (6:8; 20:4). To Rome had gone the saints and martyrs to be tormented, so that the woman and her guests at the festivals may be amused (cf. dragon, beast, woman). However, in his vision John sees the empire as already vanquished. The evil empire has done its worst and failed. Those who had deserted the ranks were never true Christians. Every fresh effort Rome makes is only another opportunity for failing more completely. The church is the only reality: the rest is sham. True believers are causing the light of Christ to shine in the darkness of superstition and unbelief. The seven letters end with the words, *He who has an ear, let him hear what the Spirit says to the churches.* That challenge is just as much ours today as it has been for all Christians down the centuries.

(D)
Visiting the sites of the seven churches

Ephesus

A visit to the main site of Ephesus begins at the Magnesia Gate. This was the main gate on the road to the east. In the later half of the second-century AD, Mamianus had the road from this gate to the temple of Artemis covered so that worshippers could walk to the temple without getting wet or sunburnt! Nearby on the other side of the road is the East Gymnasium which also dates from around the end of the second-century AD. Near the site entrance to our right is an early Christian church on which are the symbols of St Luke.

The first building of note is the Odeon which was constructed by Vedius Antonius in the second- century AD. It seated about 1,500 people and may have had a roof supported by Corinthian pillars. In front of the Odeon is a 6-metre deep gallery built at the beginning of the first-century AD and this has Ionic columns with bulls-head capitals.

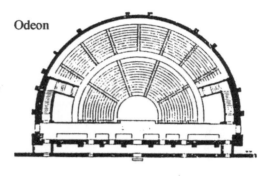

Odeon

As we begin our walk down Curetes Street we pass the Prytaneion, or town hall. were probably brought and hidden here during the reign of Constantine.

The Temple of Domitian (AD81-96) is of considerable interest. It is most likely that this was constructed at the time John wrote his letter to the church. Little remains of the temple on site, so it is well worth paying a visit to the Emperors' Cult Hall in the Selcuk Museum where the altar 7 metres long and 1.25 metres high is on display.

It is helpful to stand in Curetes Street and look towards the temple, and then try to imagine what it looked like with the huge statue of Domitian 7 metres high. Only the enormous marble head and left arm remain as a reminder of this man's megalomania.

On one side of the temple is the fountain of Pollio. A whole room in the museum is taken up with items found here, including a fine statue of a resting warrior. To the right of the temple may have been a mental health clinic. We return to Curetes Street for a look at the carved columns of Heracles and then on down the street to the second-century Temple of Hadrian (the emperor who came to Britain and built the wall). Note the decoration showing the Meander river and also the lyre.

To the right of Curetes Street we visit the public baths and toilets. The baths were built in the second century but extensively renovated in the fourth century by Schlasticia, whose headless statue stands as a memorial to her generosity. Lower down we visit the very public toilets. Not even the wealthy citizens had a private loo. During our walk down Curetes Street we have encountered the drainage system with clean water entering on one side of a building and flowing out of the other. This was the last such use before the water was channelled into the harbour.

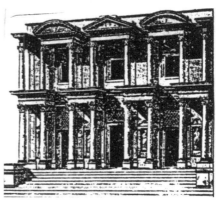

The Library of Celsus was built by Julius Aquila in AD 135. By the entrance doors stood four statues representing the virtues of knowledge and understanding. Nearby is the tomb of Celsus, who had been Roman governor of Asia. The main hall measured 11x17 metres, whilst the main facade was 10.5 metres high. The niches inside the library were for storing the scrolls. Not all was as it seemed, for an underground passageway has been found leading from the library to the brothel!

To the right of the library is the Gate of Mazeus and Mithridates. Note the inscription on it referring to the Emperor Augustus and his wife Livia, their daughter Julia and son-in-law Agrippa, reminding us that this gate was erected around the time Jesus was born.

The main Agora (market place) was reached through this gate or from the marble road that led down to the harbour. The Agora was extensively renovated in the reign of Augustus. Shops were located round the perimeter; in front of them were columns. In the centre of the agora stood a water clock.

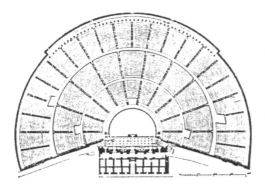

The great theatre of Ephesus was still in the process of construction when Demetrius stirred up the assembly during Paul's stay. It held at least 25,000 people on three tiers. It is important to note that the theatre was mainly used for drama and music and sometimes for public assembly, but was not used by gladiators or wild beasts.

From the theatre we can look down the Arcadian Way (530m long and 21m wide). It led down to the harbour, now crossed by the road to Kusadasi. The middle section, like the street which runs along the front of the theatre, was paved with marble and it was illuminated by street lamps at night. In the sixth century, four major pillars were erected and it is claimed that they held statues of Matthew, Mark, Luke and John.

Niemann's reconstruction of the Arcadian Way.

To the right of the Arcadian Way were a gymnasium and the harbour baths. This major complex dates from the second century but was renovated by the Emperor Constantine in the fourth century. The pillars from the baths now support the roof of the Isa Bey mosque near the church of St John.

As we leave the site we will pass the stadium. It was here that athletic games, horse and chariot racing and gladiatorial fights took place. There were covered arches for keeping the wild animals brought for even more bloodthirsty sports. The stadium dates from the time of Nero. Paul was staying in Ephesus while it was being built. It is in an elongated horseshoe shape around 250 metres long.

Before leaving the main site we will visit the church of the Council of Ephesus.

Ephesus Museum

The first room contains items found in the houses of Ephesus. The illuminated statue of Bes should not detract from such finds as the head of Tiberius—the emperor at the time of Jesus' ministry—and a first-century fresco of Socrates.

In the 'fountain findings' room note the statue of the resting warrior. Among the recent findings are examples of early Christian art. To the left of this hall are the main items of treasure. Note the silver coin from the first century with the wreathed heads of Emperor Claudius and his wife Agrippina, and on the reverse the statue and inscription 'Diana Ephesus'. In the garden are various tombs and columns, and also the reconstruction of artisans' shops from more recent times.

On leaving the garden we shall see many items of interest in the 'grave findings' hall but time should be left for the two final halls.

The Artemis Hall not only contains the beautiful statues of Artemis from the first and second centuries AD but also a variety of finds, including some priestess figurines dating from between 650-600BC at the time when King Josiah ruled Judah in the years just before the fall of Jerusalem.

The Emperor's Cult Hall contains the vast altar of Domitian, remains of his statue, the frieze from the Temple of Hadrian, and the heads of many of the emperors. Note those of Augustus and Nero.

Descriptions of the site of the Temple of Artemis, the Church of St John, the Church of the Council and the house of Mary are in earlier chapters. See index.

Smyrna

There is evidence of some early settlement from around 3,000BC and of Hittite influence from around 2,000BC, but it was the Ionians who developed Smyrna into a place that was of a size to be deemed worth capturing and destroying by King Alyattes of Lydia in the sixth century. Alexander the Great recognized its potential for trade, and one of his generals, Lysimachus, entirely rebuilt the city on a new site to the south-west and enclosed it with a wall.

In the Roman period Smyrna rivalled Ephesus and Pergamum. It was a model of town planning with straight, wide, well-paved streets laid out at right angles to each other. Golden Street ran from the harbour and temple of Cybele to the temple of Zeus at the foot of Mount Pagos and was lined with fine temples. Among the public buildings was the Homerium, built in honour of Homer the famous poet whose birthplace was claimed by Smyrna. In New Testament times Smyrna was noted for its university and medical school. Mommsen claims it was 'a paradise of municipal vanity' where earthly honour was all that counted (Rev.2:8).

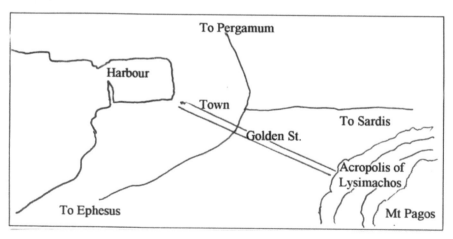

It was the first city in the area to adopt Caesar-worship. That is not out of character as the city had been adept at keeping on the winning side for several centuries. In 193BC, even before Rome controlled the area, the city had erected a temple to the deity of Rome. Caesar-worship arose out of gratitude to Rome for the prosperity the empire gave in such cities as Smyrna and was seen by the Romans as a unifying factor. It started as the worship of the goddess Roma but soon became worship of the emperor. In AD23 Smyrna was chosen from eleven contending cities for the privilege of building a temple to the Emperor Augustus and his mother. By the time of Domitian (AD81-96) it had become compulsory. Once a year each citizen had to offer a sacrifice to the emperor. Each was given a dated certificate stating that the representatives of the emperor had seen the holder make his sacrifice. This was a test of political rather than religious loyalty - the Romans did not care which God you worshipped as long as you were loyal to the state. All the Christians had to do was to place a pinch of incense on the altar and affirm 'Caesar is Lord'. But they regarded this as idolatry. Smyrna was fanatically pro-Rome and so the Christians here were in danger of *delatores* (informers), with imprisonment which usually led to death (Rev.2:10). The Jews were fairly numerous and informed on Bishop Polycarp, who had known the apostle John and who was martyred in AD155. Polycarp was given the choice of sacrificing to Caesar or being burned. He gave this answer, 'Eighty and six years have I served Christ, and he has never done me wrong. How can I blaspheme my king who saved me?' The remains of St Polycarp church are those of the oldest church in Smyrna. The church was reconstructed in 1620 by Suleiman the Magnificent.

Smyrna is also associated with other famous names in the early church. Bishop Ignatius of Antioch wrote four letters from Smyrna on his journey to martyrdom in Rome around AD120 (about 25 years after John wrote Revelation) and then, from Troas, wrote to the church at Smyrna and its bishop, Polycarp. The letters give us a helpful insight into church life of the time. Irenaeus, who died in AD202, also came from Smyrna. There are still five or six churches in Smyrna serving the various Christian communities.

Most of ancient Smyrna is under the modern city of Izmir but these areas remain.

The Agora or market place was originally constructed during the rule of Alexander the Great. What remains today, however, dates from the rebuilding of Smyrna under Marcus Aurelius after a devastating earthquake in AD178. It is bordered on the east and west by porticoes with three rows of columns, and on the north by a basilica over 170 metres long, divided into a nave and two aisles. There were galleries over the aisles and the nave was 16 metres high. It is still possible to see the interesting vaulting in the crypt.

On Mount Pagos, 200 metres high, stand the impressive ruins of a castle known as Kadife Kale, with walls built first by Lysimachus, but most of the present remains date from Byzantine and Turkish rule.

The inner harbour of New Testament times, which was protected by chains across its entrance, has been filled in and is now part of the city shopping area. The large modern city is still a major port and the second largest commercial centre in Turkey.

Pergamum

Pergamum is about 45 miles north of Smyrna and about fifteen miles from the sea on two tributaries of the Caicus river. The modern town of Bergama is built on the lower town. Bergama's main feature is the former temple, possibly used for the worship of Serapis. In the time of Constantine it was converted into a church and had a nave 230 metres long. A side chapel is now a mosque.

Pergamos, to give the city its Greek name, was founded when Lysimachus, one of Alexander's successors, settled Greek colonists. He entrusted Philetaerus with a fortune of 9,000 talents of gold worth about £3,400 million today. Philetaerus changed sides and went over to the Seleucids and then used this fortune to found the Attalid dynasty. Philetaerus built up an army and fortified the acropolis. In his arsenal were found large quantities of stone balls weighing about 50 kgs and which were ammunition for his ballistae. He was succeeded by Eumenes I (263-241BC), who broke with the Seleucids, defeating Antiochus I in battle near Sardis in 262 BC, and then by Attalus I (214-197BC), Eumenes II (197-159BC), Attalus II (159-138BC) and Attalus III (138-133BC). He bequeathed his kingdom to Rome, and so Pergamum became the capital of the Roman Province of Asia. It retained this title throughout New Testament times although the governor usually resided at Ephesus.

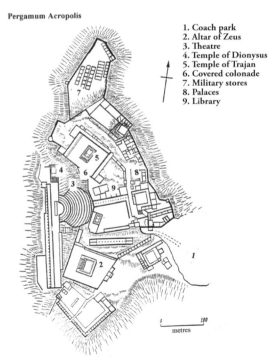

Pergamum Acropolis

1. Coach park
2. Altar of Zeus
3. Theatre
4. Temple of Dionysus
5. Temple of Trajan
6. Covered colonade
7. Military stores
8. Palaces
9. Library

The Acropolis Many of the fine buildings date from the reign of Eumenes II, who is famous for two major developments. First he constructed a syphoned water supply that was able to fill the acropolis reservoirs 300 metres above the river level. The acropolis, dominating the growing city in the valley below, was crowned by the royal palace, library, temples of Athena and Zeus, a vast terrace supported by arches, and the steepest theatre in the ancient world cascading down the side of the hill. The wonders of Pergamum are mostly to be found today in the Pergamum Museum in Berlin where the altar of Zeus measuring 36 x 34 metres has been reconstructed. This may have been alluded to in Revelation 2:13 - where Satan has his throne. Eumenes' pride and joy was the library. It was the second largest in the ancient world, containing over 200,000 books—an enormous number when they were all written by hand. At one time Eumenes tried to obtain the services of the librarian of Alexandria, for in those days Alexandria had the largest library in the world. The king of Egypt retaliated by putting his librarian in prison and stopping the supply of papyrus that was made from Nile rushes. Faced with the loss of what was regarded as being the best writing material, Eumenes sought an alternative. *Pergamene charta* was made from animal skins—it is still used today and parchment takes its name from the place where it was first made.

The Asklepion

The second part of our visit to Pergamum is at the sanctuary of Asclepios—the god of healing. It is interesting to note that Asclepios was addressed as saviour. A person wishing to be healed would lie on the temple floor while snakes, which were supposed to be the god in flesh, crawled over him. Any Christian who had read Genesis would know that the snake was the incarnation of Satan. Satan here was regarded as saviour. Incidentally, the snake portrayed on many medical emblems is that of Asclepios. The physician Galen practised at this healing centre.

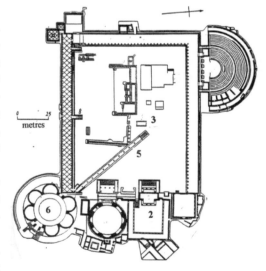

1. Sacred way	4. Theatre
2. Entrance gate	5. Covered passage
3. Sacred spring	6. Treatment centre

Thyatira

Thyatira was built on the pass connecting two important river valleys—the Hermus and the Caicus. It was in a strategic position between the two important cities of Pergamum and Sardis, which were the capitals of major kingdoms in the area. Thyatira was not a natural fortress. It was one of those towns fated to fight and then to be captured by every invader. It never controlled any territory of its own. In peaceful times down the centuries it has been an agricultural market town. That was just as true in John's day as it is today.

The town was founded as Pelopia round the shrine of the sun-god Tyrmnus. On coins this god is represented as a horseman with a double-headed battleaxe. Seleucus Nicator (300BC), Alexander the Great's successor in Syria, settled many of his Greek-Macedonian soldiers there and it became a formidable garrison for him against the kingdom of another of Alexander's successors, Lysimachus, who controlled the western part of Alexander's conquests. A century later Thyatira fell to the kingdom of Pergamum and was later bequeathed with that kingdom to Rome.

During Roman times Thyatira became an important trading centre and was permitted to issue its own currency. A sign of its importance was a visit by the Emperor Hadrian, who came to the city in AD134.

As is common with most towns that were not natural fortresses, very little remains of ancient Thyatira. There are some traces of buildings and columns for which Caracalla (AD215) received the title 'Little Benefactor'. From AD200 the city was strongly Christian and linked to the Montanist denomination. The chief remains we can see today are of one of their churches. In 1313 the neighbouring Muslim town of Manisa took over Thyatira and renamed it Ak-Hisar (white castle). Today the town of Akhisar has a population of around 70,000.

In John's day the main industry was dyeing and garment making—Lydia (Acts 16) would be a representative of a firm from Thyatira dealing in expensive cloth. Lydia had the Roman colony of Philippi as her sales pitch. The royal purple cloth of Thyatira was made using a dye from the madder root rather than the rarer shellfish used elsewhere. This meant that traders like Lydia could undercut the price of cloth from other cities. Other important industries were pottery (Rev.2:17), brass ware (Rev.2:18) and bronze armour.

Trade guilds, co-operatives or unions were very powerful and it was very hard to be employed in a trade without belonging to such a guild. They were causing considerable difficulty in the church, as Jezebel (Rev.2:20) claimed that there was no reason why a Christian should not belong to them. She claimed that it was even useful for the Christian to know the enemy (the deep things of Satan) which included meetings in a heathen temple; the heathen grace before a common meal of meat sacrificed to the honour of the patron god; and a feast that degenerated into drunkenness and immorality.

Plan of the Church at Thyatira

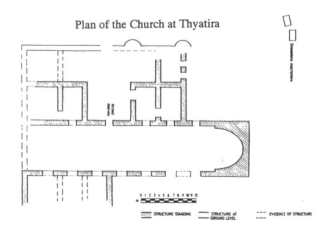

Christ in Glory - *a handbook for Christian visitors to the seven churches of the Revelation of St. John*

Sardis

Sardis is located at the crossing of five roads and so is a centre for trade. Gold dust was to be found in the River Pactolus that ran through the market place. There is something we use each day which began in Sardis, for the city is thought to be the first place in the world that minted its own coinage. Electrum gold coins and processing artefacts, some containing flakes of gold dust, can be seen in the British Museum. Small hollows, or cupels, were formed as hearths to melt down the gold dust which was purified further in small furnaces before being poured into moulds.

Cupellation and cementation processes

In the sixth century BC, Sardis was the capital city of the great Lydian empire which covered an area similar to modern-day Turkey. The mention of its king, Croesus, would send terror rushing through the minds of the Greeks. Herodotus gives an account of the downfall of this mighty empire. King Croesus enquired of the oracle at Delphi as to whether he should wage war against Cyrus, King of Persia. (This is the Cyrus who allowed the Jews to return from exile in Babylon.) He was told that if he crossed the River Halys he would destroy a mighty empire. He did - it was his own! Cyrus defeated him and Croesus fled to Sardis. There Cyrus used some eastern strategy. He knew that horses have a great dislike of the sight and smell of camels, so he commanded his cavalry to mount the camels that were normally used by the baggage corps. The Lydian horses turned and fled and so Croesus retreated to the acropolis. The Timolus range rises to 1807 metres and an outcrop of this mountain range forms the acropolis of Sardis, which was regarded as one of the best fortresses in the ancient world. All Croesus had to do was to guard a narrow strip of rock and wait for reinforcements. Yet one day in 549 a Median, Hyeroeades, saw a Lydian soldier accidentally drop his helmet over the battlements and down the cliff. He watched with amazement as the Lydian quickly climbed what was regarded as sheer rock face and recovered his helmet. That night a picked corps of troops scaled that cliff, found the top unguarded and took the garrison. Amazingly, a similar event occurred three hundred years later under the Seleucids, only this time a helmet was dropped and a Cretan, Lagorus, led the way up the cliffs.

In Roman times Sardis was in decline. It was an assize town with a certain amount of self-government. It was a trading centre for wool and cloth and the manufacture of dyes, but little more. A sign of its poverty was that after the earthquake of AD17 the Emperor Tiberius gave the city a grant of 2.5 million denarii—a labourer was paid a denarius for a day's work—and remitted tax for five years.

Sardis became an administrative capital again in AD295 when the province of Asia was divided, and in church history, a century later, Bishop Melito is described as archbishop of Lydia. However, Sardis never regained any of its former glory and the history of the church in Sardis reflects that of the letter in Revelation. It had a name for being alive but was dead. It was totally destroyed by the fierce Asiatic conqueror Tamerlane in AD1402. One interesting observation made by Sir W Ramsey a century ago was that around Sardis there was a group of people who, to avoid persecution, regarded themselves as Muslims but lived by Christian ethical standards and dress. Is this a lesson in how a pattern of life can be maintained long after spiritual life has disappeared?

Now we will look in more detail at the site of Sardis. The ruins are close to a small village and rail station of Sart and four miles from Salihli.

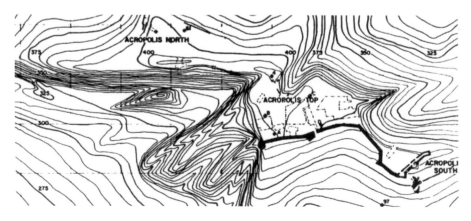

The Acropolis It takes about one hour to climb and it can prove slippery with loose gravel. The panoramic view is well worth the effort. There are some well preserved Byzantine fortifications, including a tower, gate and cisterns. Little remains from biblical times.

The Temple of Artemis King Croesus had built a temple to Cybele on the site but that temple was destroyed in 498BC. In 334BC Alexander the Great ordered a new temple to be built on the site to

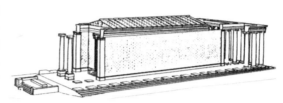

Artemis, although it appears that the forms of worship more closely resembled that of the Cybeline fertility cult. The temple was one of the seven largest buildings in the ancient world: at 99.2m by 45.7m it was more than twice the size of the Parthenon in Athens. It was never completed. When it was begun in about 200BC the intention was to built an immense Ionic *dipteros*—that is two rows of columns around the central core. The central core, including the cult statue, was completed quickly, but then construction slackened off and the temple was badly damaged by earthquakes. The temple was later used for emperor-worship, and then after Constantine a small Christian church was built in the south-east corner. By the ninth century the temple was buried by landslides so that only two columns were visible. Today one of these columns is showing the signs of recent earthquakes and it is advisable not to walk too close! The reconstruction above shows it as it was before it was closed to make way for the Christian church.

Downtown We pass this area between the temple of Artemis and the gymnasium. To the north of the area is a space that was used for the refining of gold and where the coins were made. Next to it is the Altar of Cybele but the lions on it are a modern reconstruction. At the southern end there have been several Christian churches. The one with an inverted dome—illustrated—dates from the thirteenth century. That church had five domes, but it sits directly over the nave of the fourth-century church and used some of its column bases.

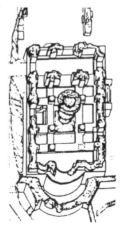

Bath-Gymnasium complex These impressive buildings are the highlight of a visit to Sardis. They cover an area of

around six acres and would have been the central feature of the Roman city. The bath-gymnasium is a fine example of the way the Romans combined these two exercise areas. Exercise and games usually preceded bathing and so the visitor entered the baths from the exercise area or *palaestra* through the marble court with its two-storyed arrangement of columns dedicated to the emperor cult. The naked bathers then entered the hot baths through a series of rooms increasing in temperature until they reached the *caldarium* (hot bath). Afterwards the bathers moved back through the tepid pools to the *frigidarium*. After this cold bath and swim, and a final massage complete with anointment and perfume, the wealthy citizens are ready for dinner. The architecture has many similarities with the facade of Roman theatres. The reconstruction incorporates about two-thirds of the original and is supported by a reinforced concrete frame. The columns now only carry their own weight.

The Jewish Synagogue The area south of the gymnasium was given over to the Jews in the third century. The synagogue is nearly 90 metres long by 20 metres wide. It is a memorial to the size, wealth and influence of the Jewish community of Sardis. Along its south wall are Jewish-owned shops and it has been possible to identify some of the trades, so giving evidence of the wide diversity of skills among that community.

Philadelphia

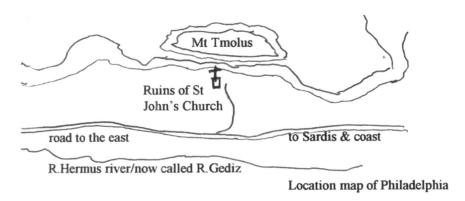

Location map of Philadelphia

Philadelphia is situated at the end of a broad valley 28 miles to the south-east of Sardis. It was a frontier town with Mysia, Lydia and Phrygia and commanded the entrance into the hills of the great highway that ran from the coast to the Middle East and beyond. It was built as a missionary city, as the last stronghold of Greek civilization before entering the wilds of Phrygia. Attulus II (150-138BC), called *philadelphus*—loyal brother—by Eumenes, King of Pergamum, founded the town and it was named Philadelphia. Shields on the coins remind us it was a military garrison.

The town is on the edge of a fertile volcanic plain known as the *katakekaumene* —the burnt land. In the past local grapes and wines were world-famous. Today, like other towns in the valley, most grapes are grown to process as sultanas. In Bible times, Philadelphia was a centre for the worship of Dionysius the god of wine. However, the town had many gods and was even nicknamed little Athens. When a prominent citizen died, people showed their regard by erecting a pillar in one of the temples and inscribing the person's name on it; hence the reference in Revelation 3:12 to a Christian being given a pillar in God's house. The hot springs in the area were also used for medicinal purposes.

Philadelphia, like most of the towns in the area, has suffered from the effects of earthquakes. It was destroyed in AD17 and given considerable help by the Emperor Tiberius. In gratitude its name was changed to Neocaesaria. In the reign of Vespasian Flavia it was given another new name—Flavia. In AD212 it had the name Neokorus, showing that it was an important centre for emperor-worship.

However, in each case it soon reverted to using its old name of Philadelphia. There is a hint of this constant name-changing during the first century when we read in Revelation 3:12 of a 'new name'. Earthquakes are also alluded to in the same verse—'you will go out no more'—as the people often fled into the open countryside and lived in temporary shelters and tents when the omens forecast an earthquake.

Philadelphia has always been a small town and is so today. The letter in Revelation is one of undiluted praise and the church there continued to flourish. In the second century, the Christian martyr Bishop Ignatius of Antioch also wrote a letter to Philadelphia in which he praises the Christians for the hospitality they had given him and urges them to grow in unity. The first bishop of Philadelphia may have been the Demetrios of 3 John 12. It was the last place in Asia to fall to the armies of Islam in 1379 and then only because it was betrayed by jealous fellow Christians in Byzantium. Until recently there was a Christian community in the town, but few remain as earlier this century many thousands of Turkish Christians were killed in severe persecution. As persecution still exists, the Christian population has emigrated or moved into safer areas. The town was renamed Alasehir (red city) by the Turks.

The remaining pillars of the massive sixth-century church of St John still bear some of the wall murals although these are not protected and so are deteriorating.

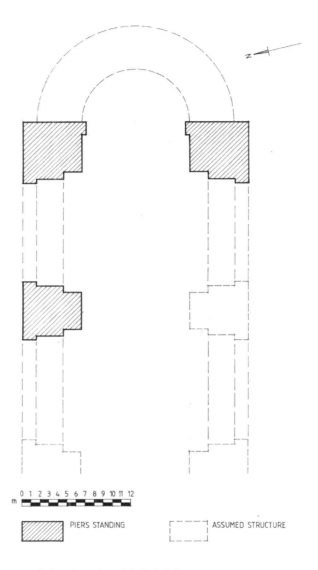

Plan of the remains of the church at Philadelphia.

This plan, along with that of the church at Thyatira was surveyed and drawn for this book by Alan Noble.

Laodicea

Laodicea was built by the Selucid Antiochus II around 230BC where the Lycus valley joins the Meander. It was named after his wife, Laodice, and was sited in hills around thirty metres above the river level. It is overlooked by mountain ranges, some reaching 2500 metres in the Baba and Khonas Dagh. The western entrance to the city was by the Ephesian gate and the eastern by the Syrian gate. Laodicea stood on the great road from Europe to the east, whilst a road ran south to the coast and another north to Philadelphia and Pergamum.

The city had no natural fortress and could never have withstood a prolonged siege, as it had to bring in all its water by aqueducts from six miles to the south. Stone pipes badly narrowed by thick deposits of calcium carbonate are still very much in evidence at the site. Some stones have a plug in the top which was removed to try and chip away at the deposits but that seems to have been a lost battle. The water arrived lukewarm. Such water was too cool for bathing, unlike that from the hot springs of Hierapolis six miles to the north, and too warm for drinking, unlike the cool springs of Colosse ten miles to the east.

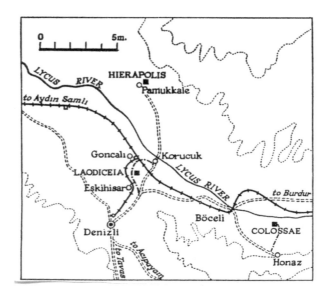

Its lack of fortifications meant that Laodicea did not grow in importance until under Roman rule. Then it outgrew most of the cities of the area and became the capital of the Cibryatic convention, which included at least twenty-five other towns in the area. Cicero, in 51BC, on his way to take up the post of governor of Cilicia, used Laodicea to cash his bank drafts and the city's banks were well known in New Testament times. He stayed in Laodicea for some months trying to build up better relations for Rome after the maladministration of his predecessor, Appius Claudius. It is interesting to note that Cicero turned down the export of wild animals from Laodicea to friends in Rome for use in public games. In AD60 a terrible earthquake destroyed the city but Tacitus the Roman historian remarks that, unlike most of the other cities in the area, Laodicea refused any state aid so that the city could be rebuilt in a splendid and extravagant style. Two examples of the affluence of this town are that in 62BC the Governor of Asia forbade the Jews to send their annual contribution of ten kilos of gold to the temple funds in Jerusalem, and the cost of building one of the large stadiums after the earthquake was funded by just one citizen, Nicostratus.

Two major sources of income were cloth and eye salve. Long-haired black sheep provided the wool for a textile trade that was well known throughout the region until the tenth century. Excavations at Aphrodisias have uncovered a price list of Laodicean textiles from the third century confirming earlier records showing the importance of this industry. Laodicea had a medical school and the names of doctors there occur on coins from the early days of the Roman empire. The Phrygian eye powder processed at Laodicea could well have come from the mineral deposits in the local hot springs. It curative value is unknown. Galen regarded it as of doubtful worth.

The time of greatest prosperity for Laodicea came towards the end of the second century. Under the Emperor Commodus the city received the coveted title of *neocorus* for its temple to the imperial cult. When Commodus died in AD 192 it lost this title and an inscription has been found with *neocorus* erased and the lesser title of 'Emperor loving' inscribed in its place.

Laodicea is mentioned in the early church history. Its bishop, Sagaris, was martyred in AD166 and Bishop Nounechios attended the Council of Nicea in AD325. At the Council of Laodicea in AD367 the church accepted twenty-six books of the New Testament as genuine but rejected the Book of Revelation with its letter critical of the Laodicean church. The city was destroyed once more by a major earthquake in AD494. It continued as a small town until the Turkish conquest in the fifteenth century. Today the site is deserted.

Sketch plan of the site of Laodicea

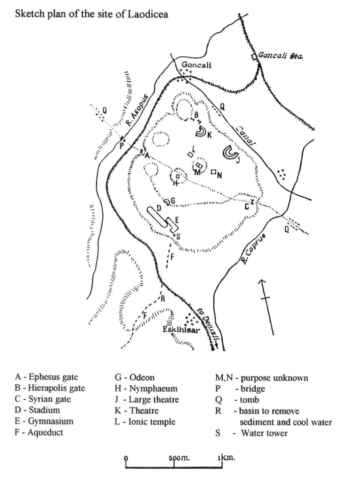

A - Ephesus gate	G - Odeon	M,N - purpose unknown
B - Hierapolis gate	H - Nymphaeum	P - bridge
C - Syrian gate	J - Large theatre	Q - tomb
D - Stadium	K - Theatre	R - basin to remove
E - Gymnasium	L - Ionic temple	sediment and cool water
F - Aqueduct		S - Water tower

The site of Laodicea at Eski Hissar has not received much attention from archaeologists. It is reached by the road from Pamukkale just before this joins the main Usak highway by turning right at the Ari Tugla-Kiremit factory. It is a good place for treasure-hunting: coins and other interesting items are scattered around the site. Much of its stone was removed and used to build the railway to nearby Denizli.

After the extensive ruins of Hierapolis, Laodicea always seems an anticlimax, yet in its day it was far grander than anything Hierapolis could offer.

The stadium was dedicated to Vespasian in AD79 and so at the time of Revelation it was resplendent in all its glory. The stadium was officially opened by the proconsul of Asia, the father of the Emperor Trajan. It is 350 metres long and forms a complete oblong track. It could therefore be used for athletics, gladiatorial shows and chariot-racing.

At the far end of the stadium are the remains of a large building. This was dedicated to the Emperor Hadrian and his wife Sabina and may have been public baths. At the southern corner there is a 5-metre high water tower. On the east side the wall has collapsed, revealing water pipes running up its core. This tower may have provided water for the baths and surrounding buildings. The main aqueduct that carried water from a spring near Denizli is clearly visible from the water tower to which it was carried under pressure over the valley.

Down the hill to the north is a small theatre (Odeon) or possibly council chamber. One hundred metres further on in that direction is the *nymphaeum*, excavated in 1962. The French found a large number of items, including a full-sized figure of the goddess Isis. Part of the building was later used as a church. Further on over the hill are two larger theatres in a reasonable state of preservation compared with the rest of the site.

Near the Syrian gate is the tomb of the philosopher Polemo. The story has it that he chose to be buried in it while still alive. 'Make fast, make fast,' he cried, 'let the sun never see me reduced to silence.'

The western or Ephesian gate was dedicated to the Emperor Domitian and so was built around the time John wrote his letter to this city. It had three arches flanked by towers. It is most likely that John's messenger entered Laodicea through this gate.

Hierapolis - Pamukkale

For centuries the thermal springs had been a centre for worship and a temple was dedicated to the local god Hieron. Major settlement on the site seems to have begun in the reign of Antiochus around 190BC, a century after developments at Laodicea. Heirapolis soon developed as an important manufacturing centre. The city was extensively damaged in the AD17 earthquake and it was nearly a century before it regained its former importance. It grew to a population of 100,000 and was an important religious, intellectual and commercial centre. Its religious and cultural festivals attracted large crowds from the surrounding towns.

The founding of the church at Hierapolis was linked to St Philip, and near the theatre Italian archaeologists have discovered his Martyrium, an octagonal chamber forming a double cross surrounded by a square that was built in the fifth century. In Paul's time the town was still recovering from the earthquake but Paul mentions in Colossians 4:13 that Epaphras was wrestling in prayer for the church in Colosse, Laodicea and Hierapolis. One assumes that the Christians there would have shared the letter written by Paul to the church at Laodicea (possibly the letter we call Ephesians) and that to Colosse.

Papias (AD60-130) was Bishop of Hierapolis. We know he was a disciple of John and companion of Polycarp. A fragment of his writings state that John told him that Mark, having become the interpreter of St Peter, had set down accurately, though not in order, everything he remembered of the words and actions of Jesus, and that Matthew composed the oracles in Hebrew. In Byzantine times Hierapolis was the seat of an Archbishop, the most famous of whom was Apollinarius.

The city was captured by the Turks in the fourteenth century and was never rebuilt after being destroyed by a major earthquake in AD1354.

Our visit begins at the **Necropolis**—city of the dead (1). This is one of the best preserved ancient cemeteries with more than a thousand tombs from the Roman, Christian and late Hellenistic periods. There is ample evidence of the size, wealth and importance of the city.

We pass the northern **Roman Baths** (2) and then the rounded towers of the gate built by Julius Frontinus in AD85 and dedicated to the Emperor Domitian (3). This ceremonial gate, with its three arches, contrasts with the fortified **Byzantine Gate** that was part of the city walls (4).

Most visitors spend their time either swimming in the hot spring water of the hotel pools or visiting the Pamukkale—cotton castle—travertines (5). Both are 'a must' and a fitting climax to any visit to the area.

If time allows the following are well worth a visit.

The **Plutonium** is on the south side of the Temple of Apollo (6). It was thought to be the entrance to the kingdom of Pluto, the god of the underworld. Anyone entering the cave died in a short time from the poisonous vapours.

The **Theatre** was built in the reign of Hadrian and provided seating for around 20,000 people (7). It is well preserved, and the third-century stage is very rich in its carvings. Some of these have been moved to the nearby museum.

Those with time and energy can continue further up the hill to the **Martyrium** of Philip (8). Only the two small chapels remain and the tomb has not yet been discovered.

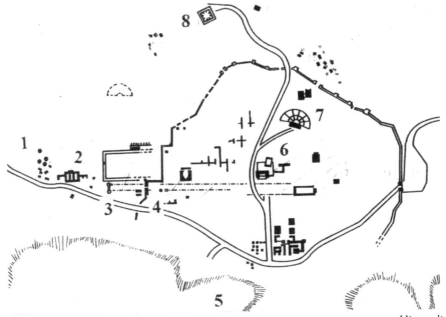

The Early Christian symbols

The fish   The Greek word for a fish is ichthus *ιχθυς*.   The letters
stand for the first letters of the Greek words for

Jesus	-	Ιησους
Christ	-	Χριστος
God's	-	Θεος
Son	-	Υιος
Saviour	-	Σωτηρ

In Ephesus we will see a more complicated symbol dating from the
second century that is made up using the same words in this way.

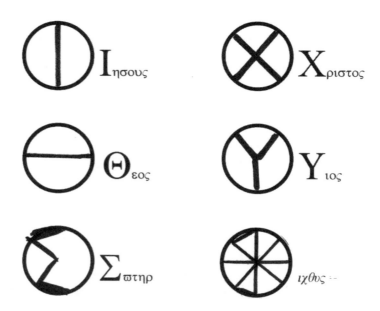

The Greek alphabet

Name	capital	lower case	like English
Alpha	A	α	a
Beta	B	β	b
Gamma	Γ	γ	g
Delta	Δ	δ	d
Epsilon	E	ε	e
Zeta	Z	ζ	z
Eta	H	η	e as in fete
Theta	Θ	θ	th
Iota	I	ι	i
Kappa	K	κ	k
Lambda	Λ	λ	l
Mu	M	μ	m
Nu	N	ν	n
Xi	Ξ	ξ	x
Omicron	O	o	o
Pi	Π	π	p
Rho	P	ρ	r
Sigma	Σ	σ ←	**s**
Tau	T	τ	t
Upsilon	Y	υ	u
Phi	Φ	φ	ph
Chi	X	χ	ch
Psi	Ψ	ψ	ps
Omega	Ω	ω	o as in tone

Notes